Helping Children
Loss a

Whether it's the grief of bereavement, the strain of divorce or the uncertainty of a new home or school, loss and change affect children in countless ways. Nevertheless, teachers and parents frequently find themselves ill-equipped to help children struggling with the difficult feelings that these situations, and others like them, bring. *Helping Children Cope with Loss and Change offers guided support for teachers, health professionals and parents.*

Designed for use with children aged 4–10, this guide offers:

- Case studies illustrating various signs of grief and loss to help the caregiver spot and manage a child's pain.
- Therapeutic stories designed to be read with the child, and with prompt questions to encourage discussion.
- Creative activities and exercises that can be developed into a therapeutic 'toolkit' to support the child and the caregivers themselves.

With chapters that move from Loss and Change to Resolution and Resilience, addressing the needs of both the children and caregivers, *Helping Children Cope with Loss and Change will be an invaluable therapeutic tool.*

Amanda Seyderhelm is an experienced play therapist and enables affected children to make sense of their feelings and to find a comfortable way to express themselves and their worries through their natural language of play.

She can be found in her Stamford practice where she offers one-to-one sessions, and at Great Ormond Street Hospital for Children where she is an ambassador. She is also the resident play therapist at the Faculty of The Child and Family Practice, a centre of excellence for child and family mental health in London. Amanda has a BA degree in English Literature and Social Anthropology, a postgraduate diploma in Play Therapy and a post-graduate certificate in systemic approaches to treating individuals, families and organisations from The Tavistock and Portman NHS Foundation Trust. She is a member of Play Therapy UK and The Association for Family Therapy and Systemic Practice.

Helping Children Cope with Loss and Change

A Guide for Professionals and Parents

Amanda Seyderhelm

Routledge
Taylor & Francis Group

LONDON AND NEW YORK

First published 2020
by Routledge
2 Park Square, Milton Park, Abingdon, Oxon OX14 4RN

and by Routledge
52 Vanderbilt Avenue, New York, NY 10017

Routledge is an imprint of the Taylor & Francis Group, an informa business

© 2020 Amanda Seyderhelm

British Library Cataloguing-in-Publication Data
A catalogue record for this book is available from the British Library

Library of Congress Cataloging-in-Publication Data
A catalog record has been requested for this book

ISBN: 978-1-911186-28-1 (pbk)
ISBN: 978-0-429-28545-5 (ebk)

Typeset in Frutiger and Sabon
by Servis Filmsetting Ltd, Stockport, Cheshire

Dedication
For my Dad,
you are the best there is.

For all
the quiet ones,
the outsiders,
those who wish they could be still and quiet
and those who want to roar …
I hear you.
I see you.
This book is for all of you.

Bird Wings by Rumi

Your grief for what you've lost
lifts a mirror up to where you're
bravely working.
Expecting the worst, you look, and
instead, here is the joyful face
you've been wanting to see.
Your hand opens and closes, and opens
and closes. If it were always a
fist, or always stretched open, you
would be paralysed.
Your deepest presence is in every
small contracting and
expanding, the two as beautifully
balanced and co-ordinated as
bird wings.

Contents

Foreword

Many years ago, my colleague Sophie Webb was working with a child whose mother had died two days before his third birthday. He spent his birthday gently caring for a doll. He bathed the doll, dressed her, took her for a walk in the park and even made sure she was with him when he used the potty. When Sophie asked him whether he would like to give his doll a name, he replied 'Mum'. This type of symbolic representation is common throughout children's play, but in this case the child is clearly using the doll as an integral part of his grieving process. In her reflective diary Sophie commented that one of the most obvious, but nonetheless vital messages to come out of this was 'he still needs his mum around'.

Freud tells us that one of the benefits of play lies in the process of reconciliation. The suggestion is that children do this very naturally in their play. In Freud's thinking, children who do this are engaged in two intertwined therapeutic processes. Firstly, they are deepening their understanding of what has happened to them, and secondly, they are metaphorically taking control of the event. Returning to the above example, Sophie also comments that this child is 'trying to speak to us through his play' and suggests 'we need to find structured and unstructured ways of helping him'. That is exactly what Amanda Seyderhelm sets out to achieve in this book.

Of course, the death of a loved one is the most common ways in which we think of loss in childhood, but the subject is so much more complex than that. Children experience loss and change in all sorts of ways, and the feelings engendered by those events are often akin to bereavement. In this book the reader is introduced to the concept that childhood grief follows an identifiable pattern. However, the author is careful to view this from the standpoint of the child, rather than the 'expert' adult. She also highlights the distinction between the role of those who come into contact with children on a daily basis, such as teachers, and those who work with children in a more specialized way. The former, she says, are likely to be the people who first identify children who are struggling to cope with emotional issues. All being well they will refer such children on to specialists, such as pastoral staff, counsellors and play therapists. These are the people whose job it is to help children cope with loss, change and bereavement.

Sadly, everyone involved in this process is at risk of burnout – teachers and specialists alike. This may happen because the issue of childhood loss is not recognized by senior managers, with the consequence that the teacher is not properly supported. It may be that there are no specialists available, and so teachers feel compelled to try to help the children themselves. It may simply be a question of a lack of adequate education and training. It might even be a result of the adults' own unresolved issues from a past trauma. Whatever the reasons, the author offers a pathway towards resolution. Indeed, the book addresses the very specific needs of the workers by asking and answering a number of key questions, such as how can we help these professionals with their communication skills, how can we bolster their ability to attain and retain effective relationships, and how can we help them to develop resilience and guard against burnout?

Seyderhelm provides a substantial and very practical guide for such people – initially by exploring the role of therapeutic stories in the grieving and reconciliation process. She then provides examples of approaches that pastoral staff within the education system might employ to address the emotional needs of a grieving child. A number of case studies are also explored to illustrate how the process might work. This is all done within a four-phase framework of loss, change, resolution and resilience. Let us hope that the outcome of this book is for the emotional needs of children to be taken more seriously so that practitioners are no longer working with one hand tied behind their back.

Professor Fraser Brown
Childhood Development and Playwork Team
Leeds Beckett University

Preface

Anyone who says you can write a book in 10 days is lying! *Helping Children Cope with Loss and Change* has been years in the making, inspired by and conceived after the publication in 2012 of my picture book for grieving children, *Isaac and the Red Jumper*.

To follow on from a successful and award-winning career in Oxford academic publishing wasn't an easy task, but a major loss of my health changed the course and direction of my life, forcing me to reconsider and rethink just how I did want to live and work. This labyrinth-like examination led me back to an early insight I had gained as a teenager while reading the book, *DIBS: In Search of Self* by the American Play Therapist, by Virginia Axline. The book was one of several keys I used to unlock the inner doors I had unconsciously closed off and opened my inner eye to realise that yes, *now* I was ready to train as a Play Therapist. However, this wasn't quite the 'fun and games' that the name implied, and I quickly learned, under the expert and wise tutelage of Monika Jephcott's Academy of Play and Child Psychotherapy, that playing, in a child-centred way, meant exploring my inner child and all of her territory – narratives and stories first – because how could I expect a child to explore their pain if I hadn't explored my own? My role as a therapist was and is to be able to bear what my clients find unbearable and together, to discover a meaning that makes sense to the child.

Training is one thing, *becoming* is quite another matter, and it took several years of treating children in Primary Schools until I saw a pattern emerging in my clinical practice which brought everything into focus – loss was central to all conditions I treated in children. The causes of loss were different – death, divorce and disease were the top three, along with a sense of homelessness felt in fostered and adopted children – but some kind of heartbreak caused by loss was *always* at the centre of the child's struggle, together with the deepest longing for belonging. After several years in private practice, I came to see that this longing for belonging wasn't unique to young primary school aged children, in fact, it was often deeply buried inside the adults inside all social networks a child touched – families, schools, local authorities and General Practice.

No-one seemed immune from loss, there was no pill, no tincture to cure the pain which, if ignored, could turn into burn out. In the words of the poet Robert Frost, 'the best way out is through'.

With this in mind and to ease and signpost your passage through the book, I have included tools from my therapeutic practice and adapted these for the busy teacher and teaching assistant in the classroom, the busy parent at home, the busy Social and Family Support Worker and busy GP, to help support a child's emotional development, as they move through life's inevitable stages of loss and change.

I have been inspired in my work by Rachel Pinney, founder of The Children's Trust who pioneered therapeutic approaches to children's development in the 1960s which she termed

Creative Listening and Children's Hours, together with Virginia Axline, the Play Therapist who introduced me to the concepts of active listening and accepting the child 'as is' – unconditionally, no matter what. These two concepts have no doubt been the most influential in shaping me as a Play Therapist. I have found that whatever difficulty or challenge the child is facing, when I let them know that I accept them as they are, and wherever they are, this opens a door into the child's world. This is above all the first thing I do when meeting new children. Once they realise that I am not judging them, they relax and begin to introduce me to their world. When I first introduced these concepts to busy social workers and family support workers they found it very challenging to keep their judgments and personal feelings in check, and working in this way felt awkward. However over time, and after experimenting with these concepts through the creative arts mediums, they learnt how to hold and contain their personal feelings which made room for the child. I believe these therapeutic concepts are helpful for teachers, parents and Social and Family Support Workers to learn too, and so I introduce them to you here in this book, along with some creative exercises.

I am aware that doing some of these exercises may open your inner eyes and doorways – I encourage you not to shy away from these because behind them, for sure, will be insights that will change the way you think and live. However, if you would like support while working through some of these exercises, I invite you to contact me directly through website: www.amandaseyderhelm.com

Amanda Seyderhelm,
Helping Children Smile Again
2020

Acknowledgements

Helping me to 'make my way through' were people from different backgrounds and professions, all of whom have found their way to my door and, in some cases, to my heart as well.

Therefore, my thanks and deepest gratitude go to:

- The late, great Rachel Pinney, the British doctor who pioneered therapeutic approaches to children's development in the 1960s which she termed Creative Listening and Children's Hours – you opened the door for my curiosity to blossom.
- Virginia Axline, the American clinical psychologist who showed me what I was born to do and kept me awake through the night, aged 16, while I read her pioneering book *DIBS: In Search of Self* about the little boy everyone thought had a cognitive and emotional disorder but who was really struggling to express himself and cope with his feelings. Dibs was subsequently tested at the end of his play therapy and found to score in the extremely gifted range, with an IQ of 168 on the Stanford-Binet Intelligence Test. There is always hope.
- Monika Jephcott, CEO of Play Therapy UK, who set me on my path to becoming a play therapist, and whose model and high standards of practice continue to inspire, to guide and to drive me.
- Karen O'Neill and Kate McKairt, my course directors at the Academy of Play and Child Psychotherapy, for my postgraduate Certificate in Therapeutic Play Skills and Diploma in Play Therapy, for holding the spaces for exploration and development, and teaching me a child-centred therapeutic framework that acknowledged, respected and honoured the child's voice.
- Christine Morris, wise and gifted clinical supervisor, you have guided me throughout my training and practice in ways too numerous to acknowledge here. We know what they are. From you I learnt important lessons: how to take five minutes before jumping in anywhere, and when 'enough really *is* enough'.
- Tim Cox, Deputy Head at The Malcolm Sargent Primary School, Stamford, Lincs, you hired me on the spot to do my training placement at the school, and I spent four very happy and rewarding years learning my craft of play therapy and the art of what it *really* takes to work in and to lead a primary school – thank you and *all* your staff for trusting me with your children and helping me to establish a play therapy provision in Lincolnshire.
- The children at The Malcolm Sargent Primary School, Stamford, you came into the 'uniform room' with me each week and told me your stories through the play therapy mediums of art, music, movement, puppet theatre and sand. The privilege of hearing your stories was all mine. I am the play therapist I am because of you.
- The parents at The Malcolm Sargent Primary School, Stamford, you graciously consented for me to work with your children, and talked candidly about your family struggles and heartache. I applaud your courage and thank you warmly for opening your hearts and families to

me and for being willing to try out different home-based strategies to support your children's emotional wellbeing.

- The SENCOs, teachers, teaching assistants and parents at the primary schools in Lincolnshire, Leicestershire and Rutland: Copthill Primary School, Whissendine Primary School, Oakham Primary School, Blue Coats Primary School, Kendrew Barracks Primary School, Uppingham Primary School, Oundle Primary School, Ketton Primary School – thank you for recognizing the children with a need for emotional support (especially the quiet ones!) and for referring your children to me for play therapy; for listening and taking on board my recommended classroom changes to support and develop their resilience.

- Kate Wells and Neil Martin, managers of the Children and Family Support Team at Leicester City Council, together with team-member social workers and family support workers Steph, Lisa, Grace, Claire and Sam – *thank you* for commissioning me to deliver the Containment Day trainings which support the mental and emotional wellbeing of the team while you work at the coalface of child and family support. Thank you for forming the circle with me and for always, *always* being willing to step inside that circle and use your voice to express both your losses and wins. Together we have set the standard for this training to be rolled out nationally!

- Jamie Wilcox and Patti Hogan, Head and Deputy Head of the Volunteering Team at Great Ormond Street Hospital for Children – *huge* thanks for inviting me to work at GOSH; your encouragement and support helped me and my team to establish The Craft Station as a vibrant and welcoming space to support outpatients through the creative arts to cope with and ease their anxiety and stress while they awaited medical treatment.

- The children and families at Great Ormond Street Hospital for Children who visited my team at The Craft Station – you truly inspired us with your courage and big hearts; thank you for all your creations, some of which have made it into this book.

- Rukiya Jemmott, my academic course director of systemic studies at The Tavistock and Portman NHS Foundation Trust, and Stephen Mills, systemic psychotherapist and tutor – thank you both for showing me how working systemically not only leaves no voice out but also makes provision to *include all* voices.

- Penny Lockwood, Manager of TreeTops Counselling and Emotional Support Service for bereaved adults and children for offering me a place to see bereaved children.

- Robert (Bob) Campbell, MD of Blackwells Oxford, for guiding me in my publishing career at Blackwells in Oxford, where I learnt, amongst *many* things, to master the art of the pitch!

- Kathleen Furin, my editor at Author Accelerator – WE did it!

- Professor Fraser Brown for writing the Foreword to this book.

- Ben Hulme-Cross, Commissioning Editor at Speechmark: 'You've got something much bigger here, do you want to write that?' you said. Thank you for your vision.

- Katrina Hulme-Cross, Publisher at Speechmark, I greatly appreciated your understanding and patience while I wrote this book, and value your expertise and wisdom. Our journey together is just beginning and I'm excited to see where this takes us!

Introduction

This book aims to give teaching professionals a practical story-making guide to enable them to help children cope with loss and change and show them how to avoid compassion fatigue by creating relationships based on compassion.

It is the first book to focus on the emotional and psychological needs of both professionals and children in primary schools. It is both a preventative and targeted resource for teachers, social workers and pastoral staff (pupil mentors, counsellors, TAs, SENDCOs and the Senior Leader Team (SLT)) respectively.

Too many children feel lonely and isolated in their grief, and their mental health suffers due to a lack of solid supports. These children are then at risk of not achieving their full potential academically and socially. If professionals are given these tools they will be better able to support children through the daunting challenges posed by having to deal with loss and grief.

Why this resource?

Currently there are four unmet needs in the field of childhood loss and bereavement:

- Limited awareness amongst professionals about signposting childhood loss and bereavement in the classroom due to the absence of bereavement training.
- A therapeutic storytelling resource for pastoral and other professional staff to use with bereaved children.
- An awareness of how to deal with unresolved adult grief so that it does not get in the way of dealing with childhood grief.
- Confusion about how to develop professional resilience and best practice to manage the teacher/parent/multiagency relationship, without burnout and compassion fatigue.

The consequences of these unmet needs

- The majority of children don't have their grieving process validated because they fall through the signposting net in the classroom, which contributes to their lack of emotional resilience, a optimism and deteriorating mental health.

- Professionals burn out as a result of 'over-caring' and develop compassion fatigue which affects their performance.

Aims and scope

- To help bereaved children cope with their loss and build emotional resilience by processing their grief through therapeutic story.
- To help professionals build rapport with children and gain a deeper understanding of the children's emotional world to enable them to communicate more effectively with the children.
- To enable professionals to skill up regarding the signposting of bereaved children, and the processing of their own unresolved grief to avoid this getting in the way of helping the bereaved children.
- To build professional resilience and avoid compassion fatigue.

Why now?

- The Department for Education announced in May 2016 a fund of £6 million for 'character grants' aimed at schools promoting traits such as resilience and respect.
- Childhood bereavement statistics show that one child in every classroom has experienced a loss of some sort. Teachers are not trained to identify the grief stages and signs.
- Children may experience multiple losses.
- Professionals are expected to provide pastoral care, yet are not trained to deliver the provision.
- Schools have become the unofficial gatekeepers of childhood mental health. This means that teachers need effective classroom management tools to support children who are going through loss and change.

Other children will experience different types of losses that mirror a bereavement in terms of the disappearance of something cherished such as a person, possession or property.

For example these losses include:

- Divorce
- Moving house
- Moving schools
- Moving country
- Friends and family move away
- A parent goes to jail
- Being taken into care
- Loss of a well-liked member of staff
- Losing a sibling through separation during the fostering and adoption process
- Domestic abuse – currently the child protection register has over 50,000 children identified as needing protection from abuse in the UK. The NSPCC has reported that for every child identified as needing protection from abuse, another eight children are suffering abuse.

This book is important because loss and change can lead to challenging behaviours both in and out of the classroom. By learning to support children emotionally and helping them to process the loss, we can alleviate some of the stress these challenging behaviours cause and improve the classroom culture.

Professionals are expected to provide emotional support yet are not trained to provide children with the space and framework to learn how to cope with and learn from their loss. Classroom teachers aren't mental health specialists and their main role is to be able to signpost mental distress, offer early evidence-based support, and know when to refer on for more specialist care and interventions.

This resource will enable teachers to explore possible reactions in response to loss, and to signpost when a child needs specialist bereavement care and therapeutic interventions. The majority of children should be treated within the school environment but if children are cutting themselves or engaging in other dangerous behaviours, a specialist referral should be made.

This resource will explain how to signpost bereaved children and provide them with creative therapeutic support to help them cope with expressing their grief.

Where do I start?

The first step in supporting grieving children has to do with creating the space between you and the children, so that you can acknowledge and accept, without judgement, their loss, which will lead you to determine the action necessary to help support them in adjusting and transitioning through their loss and change.

I teach how to create this space between parent and child and teacher and child, for the truth to emerge – this book will offer a toolkit and then give teachers directions about how to impart this in the classroom through a toolkit they can use both in and out of the classroom. I will also present cases from my clinical play therapy practice and my experiential training workshops that I deliver to teachers and local authority family social and support workers in how to support children struggling with bereavement, loss and change.

A resource to help professionals assess childhood grief

Bereavement training is exclusive to bereavement counsellors, which means that other professionals are left to figure out how to deal with childhood grief themselves. Given the pressure on these pastoral care professionals to deliver results, childhood loss and bereavement are not prioritized or assessed as a need.

This resource will educate professionals about signposting and providing pastoral support for the grieving child using therapeutic story.

A resource to build professional resilience

Teachers need to learn how to keep the grieving parents 'on side' by helping them feel valued and heard. Learning how to have compassionate conversations will help professionals deal with difficult conversations efficiently and effectively to build rapport and trust, while not becoming drained or overwhelmed (also known as 'compassion fatigue').

Read the book before reading the stories

Professionals must read the Guide before reading any of the stories to children, because this will teach them how to offer the children a more empathic response. They will learn how to answer any questions, and if handled sensitively, a child's questions can lead to them opening up about their circumstances, but this must not be pushed. Additionally, gaining insight into the psychological messages in the book will help professionals to engage with the creative resources recommended in the book.

To cope with loss and change, and help a child 'smile again', a professional needs to learn four principles:

- Active listening
- Reflection of feelings and acknowledgement of the unsaid loss
- Identification of the child's story narrative
- Acceptance without judgement of the child's ending.

I explain why it's relevant to understand the impact of stress on early brain function, and the ways in which this may present itself in early years children, what to look out for, and how best to support effective functioning in the classroom – I use Jack Shonkoff's research, *From Neurons to Neighbourhoods*, to show why.

Therapeutic play and story-playing give bereaved children the medium through which to create optimism and self-resilience because it gives them an opportunity to discover themselves in the story, to discover meaning, not only of themselves but also to make sense of the events happening around them and to them. Martin Seligman argues that the optimistic child has a sense of mastery, which is derived from being in control, being positive and not being passive; he is able to reflect on his world, be curious, challenge reality as in, establish the facts, all of which help him to overcome adversity.

Bereavement brings change, and simply being able to identify with the character in the story, to feel what it's like to take the 'hero's journey', and not merely be the victim of the change, a passive bystander, gives them skills to build optimism, and resilience.

Teachers are busy people, so at the end of each story there is a toolkit which can easily be incorporated into the classroom. When children need time out, this is a useful toolkit to use with them. You can set them up within ten minutes.

The child-centred framework, outlined by Capra and Rogers, takes into account the children's relationship to their families, community and wider society. Children don't exist in a vacuum; first they belong to themselves, have an identity and sense of self and of who they are, have parents, families, a community, and hopefully a connection to wider society in which they make a contribution, find their place and activate their gifts.

This book takes a child-centred approach, as does my play therapy practice, which means the child sets the agenda, drives the bus and has control, all of which can be very scary for new patients who suddenly find themselves standing alone with me in the play therapy room. The three of us (patient, play therapist, and the toys) stand together in the room, and begin a journey, start to form a relationship, tell stories, get to know one another – the child's inner and outer worlds are expressed in that room through the toys, and our relationship.

Learning who they are, and where they fit into their families and community is a huge ask, as well as the most worthwhile work the child will ever do; done right, it will help the child to navigate choppy waters, and learn how to steer their ship to calmer shores. Children who start play therapy usually have experienced some kind of trauma, their ship has sunk,

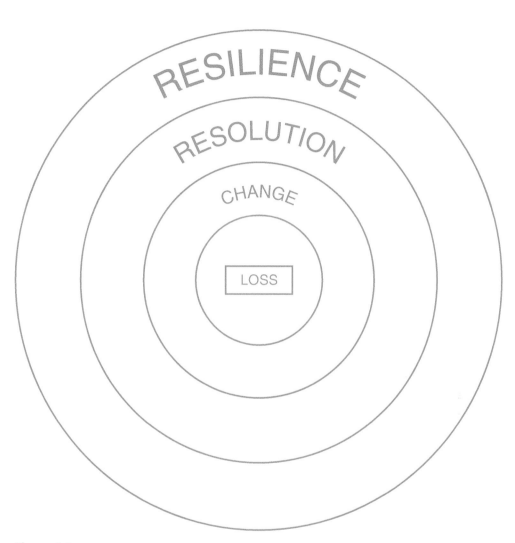

Figure 1.1

someone else has taken control and hurt them, they have suffered a bereavement and loss, and feel lost to themselves because they don't know how to make sense of the change, and their feelings are all in a muddle. My job is to help them reconnect with themselves, find those missing parts of their identity through expressing their feelings, and learn how to manage, contain and hold them without becoming overwhelmed. Bereavement and change can be very scary and difficult for children because primary school-aged children don't have the cognitive development to articulate and challenge their thoughts and feelings, so they act out. To reconnect, we tell stories, and through the stories, we make these connections. This is a thrilling dance, one in which the children star and shine, and when they fall, and they inevitably will when they collide with their hurt and pain, they learn how to cope by accessing inner resources they didn't know they had. This is where they start to overcome and accept change.

For parents

You have the choice to sit down and read the story with your child or, if you are short of time, you can use the drilling down and reflecting technique referred to above. If you are sitting down to read the story I recommend that you do this with your phone and TV switched off. Settle down in a quiet environment when you know you won't be disturbed. If you have other children, ask for support from them to remain out of the room while you do the reading. This will improve the quality of your ability to really listen and hear your child's responses to the story, and for you to be able to fully engage your attention with them. Your child will definitely pick up the fact that you are fully attentive which will help them to relax and open up to you. You may find that you have to read the story several times before this happens, so don't worry if on the first attempt you encounter resistance – whatever happens, treat this as useful feedback and see it as an opportunity to learn more about how your child is feeling. There is no right nor wrong feedback. Reading the story is an opportunity for you to deepen the trust between you and your child and the more this happens the more you will learn.

The cycle of loss and change

Loss = Change, which *provokes* Resolution and a chance to build Resilience.

The first thing that happens after we experience a loss is change. Immediately our life looks and feels different. Right here is a moment of choice. We can either lean into the change, which at first feels like a void, the thing that's left after loss, where we might feel a great sense of disconnection, or we can protect ourselves by building stronger defences around our feelings. If we lean into change, we encounter opportunities to resolve and make peace with this loss: tie up loose ends, repair damaged relationships – this is where we start to experience the new stage of 're-connection', where we aren't numbing our feelings, we are able to acknowledge and accept them, which in turn enables us to help others cope with their loss and change. This is how we build resilience.

Figure 1.1 can be used in the classroom to explain the cycle of loss and change to pupils.

Chapter 1

Loss

We are powerless to control the losses and catastrophic events our children need to experience, but by honouring their inner wisdom, providing mentors, and creating safe spaces for expression, we can empower them to become more capable, more caring, human beings.

Linda Goldman, *Children Also Grieve*, 2005

Background and rationale

Research figures published by Child Bereavement UK (online) show that:

- 92% of children and young people will experience a 'significant' bereavement before the age of 16;
- up to 70% of schools have a bereaved pupil on their roll;
- 1 in 29 school-age children will have been bereaved of a parent or sibling.
- 1 in 16 has been bereaved of a close friend.

That is one bereaved child in every classroom!

Context

Childhood Bereavement UK states that bereaved children report experiences of being bullied as a result of their bereavement and can also experience difficulties with concentration and a lack of interest in school. Bereavement can also interrupt a pupil's school attendance and may also be a factor in behaviour in school.

What can schools do?

The purpose of this book is to give school staff a toolkit so that they feel more confident and equipped to identify and help a child who is going through a bereavement, loss or change.

How children and young people grieve

The way children grieve will to some extent be determined by their attachment style. Research completed by Dr Colin Murray Parkes shows us that the attachment style and vulnerability that is evident in childhood continues into adult life and may have an impact on the way individuals react to losses such as bereavements in adult life. How our attachments develop in childhood can influence how far we can trust ourselves and others in our life. Crucially our attachment style may affect our ability to form coping strategies when an important close relationship is lost.

Dr Parkes studied a sample of 278 individuals referred to him by a general physician, often with loss related problems. His work discusses attachment styles and describes them as being:

Secure: Those whose parents provided security grow up trusting themselves and others, which enables them to be able to tolerate separations without suffering high anxiety. Although they may struggle with unexpected losses, they may cope well with the changes the losses bring and use them to discover new meaning.

Anxious/Ambivalent: Those whose parents were anxious, overprotective and/or insensitive to meeting their child's need for independence, tend to grow up being anxious, with low self-confidence and with a tendency to cling to their parents. They tend to struggle with separating from their parents and their relationships in adult life may contain a lot of conflict. After a bereavement their anxiety dominates their behaviour and they may cling to those trying to support them. Children with this attachment style may show a tendency to form dependent relationships which teachers need to be aware of.

Avoidant: Those whose parents were intolerant of intimacy and expressing emotion learn to be inhibited from emotional displays and to be independent from an early age. They may become intolerant of intimacy which can complicate their adult relationships. Following bereavement, they tend to be inhibited in their grief which may then show up in distorted ways. They are often hard on themselves for their inability to express their feelings, and may respond positively to a relationship which allows them to be expressive.

Disorganized: Those whose parents' emotional needs made it impossible for them to respond consistently to their child's needs may grow up feeling helpless about their own needs and distrusting themselves and others. Bereavement can panic them and also give them a chance to discover that not everyone will let them down.

Teachers can provide children with the secure base that makes them feel safe enough to face the struggles associated with loss and change that can make them feel very unsafe.

Grief work is a wholehearted challenge, affecting us physically, emotionally, psychologically and spiritually. It is heroic work because it takes courage and tenacity to take the challenge on. I liken this work to heroic work, as in the hero's journey. The hero's journey is the common template that involves a hero who goes on an adventure, and faced with a crisis, finds the resources to win, and returns home changed or transformed. Rooted in narratology and comparative mythology, it was adapted by Joseph Campbell and other scholars to describe man's universal spiritual quest for understanding themselves through story.

For grieving children in the 4–10 age group, who struggle to express their grief verbally, the hero's journey is a practical framework in which they can understand their grief.

I believe the task of healing from bereavement is for children to find their voice, which may have been hidden underneath fear and confusion, and depending on the circumstances of their loss, shock. Finding their voice involves them making sense of their grief and loss, and the best way to do this is through metaphorical story, set within a hero's journey framework.

In the traditional hero's journey, the main character finds a mentor who advises him to discover his own resources. In my stories, this mentor character is often a parent, friend or teacher. In doing this I hope to encourage this audience to engage with the children in the storytelling. There are adult messages for them in the stories.

In my practice, I provide a space where the child's narrative can be understood and heard through the power of play. Landreth (2002, p. 304) reminds us that toys are children's words, and play is their language. Therefore a narrative approach to play therapy can be construed simply as play therapy itself wherein the therapist respects the forms of expression of those narratives which are available to the child through the Play Therapy toolkit. I agree with Cantor (2007, p. 12) that 'narrative therapists seek to re-author the dominant problem-saturated stories in a client's life'. The study of therapeutic storytelling illuminates that for many clinical approaches, both classic and modern, storytelling frequently involves the creation of a new story. It's the new story that I am interested in helping bereaved children find. Bereaved children recreate their story, and the therapeutic stories in this book will give you the framework within which to explore the bereaved child's grief.

How children understand death at different ages

Grief reactions may not be immediately obvious to teachers and caregivers. Children and young people may put up a good front pretending they are coping better than they actually are, in order to protect those around them. Their feelings may be bottled up and understanding this may happen is essential when supporting children. Making time and space for children to express these feelings is vital.

Children can sense loss from an early age. Their level of understanding develops alongside their cognitive development.

Infants (birth to 2 years)

A baby has no understanding of death or dying but will be aware of a separation from the person to whom they have an attachment. Their reaction to this separation could be expressed by increased crying, decreased responsiveness, erratic feeding and disrupted sleep patterns.

Preschool-age children (2–5 years)

Children believe that death is reversible and expect the deceased to return. This is the 'magical thinking' stage where the world is understood as a combination of reality and fantasy. At this stage children are naturally egocentric and may develop unexpressed guilt as a result of thinking that they caused the person to die and if they are 'good enough' the deceased person will return to them. Children struggle to grasp abstact concepts like death, which is why it's important to speak clearly about death so that these fantasies of the dead person coming back to life are not indulged. To try and make sense of events children may often repeat the same questions. We often see children at this stage worrying about who will take care of them and about being abandoned. They will struggle to put their feelings into words and instead react to loss by acting out through behaviours like irritability, aggression, physical symptoms, sleep difficulties, or regression (bed-wetting or thumb-sucking, babyish language and temper tantrums). They could also make over-anxious attachments to familiar adults to try and ease their loss.

Primary school-age children (6–12 years)

Children start to understand the permanence and irreversibility of death and something that is part of the natural cycle of life. In spite of this they may still at times use 'magical thinking' and see death as a bit 'SPOOKY' which may lead them to develop a curiosity in the more morbid aspects of death, such as what happens to the body and how it decomposes. They may think of the dead person as a spirit, a ghost, an angel or a skeleton. They do start to become less egocentric and more aware of the feelings of those around them. Physically they may complain of headaches, tummy aches, which are physical manifestations of their emotional pain that they cannot yet fully verbally articulate. They may experience a range of emotions including guilt, anger, shame, anxiety, sadness and worry about their own mortality. They may experience difficulty expressing these feelings verbally and they may act them out behaviourally as school phobia, poor school performance, aggression and withdrawal from their friends.

Grief processes

Grief is a reaction to any form of loss.

Bereavement is the process of recovering from the death of a loved one. Both encompass a range of feelings from sadness to anger, and the process of adapting to a significant loss varies from one person to another, depending on his or her background, beliefs, relationship to what was lost, and other factors.

Childhood bereavement differs from adult bereavement because young children do not have the cognitive development and language to express their grief verbally. Therefore, engaging them through therapeutic story gives them a safe distance to explore their feelings through metaphor.

Models of grief

Freud (1917) originated the notion of, 'grief work', the idea that we must work through grief to overcome it. Bowlby (1980) incorporated this idea into his attachment theory, for the purpose of 'rearranging representations of the lost person, and relatedly, of the self' (Stroebe and Schut, 1999). This enabled the breaking of affectional bonds (Bowlby, 1969), and the relocation of the deceased so that adjustment could be made to the physical absence of this person in life. This model has been criticized by other theorists, particularly Worden (1991) who reformulated the grief process in terms of distinct tasks. In all of this, it is important to note that we must not simply extend the adult models, stages and tasks of grief to children, because we know that young children have not developed cognitively to the point where they can verbally express their feelings in a similar way to adults. This is why the framework of therapeutic storytelling allows bereaved children to develop their own understanding of their grief, in their own language of play and story-making.

My approach to working with grief aligns closely with Neimeyer's reconstruction in the wake of loss, in which 'a central process in grieving is the attempt to reaffirm or reconstruct a world of meaning that has been challenged by loss' (Neimeyer, 2001). Working with bereaved children, we do this by learning to explore a narrative within the context of metaphor and therapeutic story, to help the children find their own meaning; this enables children to build a safe internal modelling of the deceased, while also exploring ways to rebuild their life after loss. This helps them to feel more secure both internally and externally, as they go about their daily lives.

This approach also makes room for a more culturally diverse range of grieving. Different conceptualizations of what is acceptable or 'healthy' ways of coping with loss are to be found in non-Western cultures (Stroebe & Schut, 1999; Stroebe & Stroebe, 1987). For example in some Aboriginal tribal peoples, mutilating the body, or tearing of the hair is considered to be a normal way of working through grief (Stroebe & Stroebe, 1987).

Some cultures show little or no evidence of 'working through' patterns, because this would be considered detrimental to the health of the bereaved (among the Muslim community of Bali, Wikan, 1988.)

The stage model of loss

Perhaps the most well-known model demonstrating ways to process loss is **Elizabeth Kubler-Ross's** stage model of loss, which emerged out of a research project involving terminally ill patients (Kubler-Ross, 1982). While Kubler-Ross believed these stages to be universal, more recent research shows that not everyone goes through each stage, and the order may be different for each person. This model reflects a time when talking about death and dying was considered a taboo and gave us a framework in which to start to talk about both.

The five stages are:

1. Denial – individuals believe the loved one is still alive, and cling to a false reality that the death is a mistake.
2. Anger – individuals start to get frustrated: 'Why me? It's not fair!'
3. Bargaining – negotiating with God to bring the loved one back.
4. Depression – mourning for losses.
5. Acceptance – realizing that death is inevitable and final.

Children may also move through the stages of shock, denial, a growing awareness and finally, acceptance of the death (Ward, 1993). However, these stages are not always completed in a linear way, a process which reflects the ups and downs reported by many bereaved, where working through grief has been likened to riding sea-waves: there are calm as well as stormy times (Heegard, 1991). We often hear the phrase, 'my grief comes over me in waves'; this is what is being referred to Parkes, 1986 explains that the bereaved may well return to earlier stages of grieving before moving on to resolution.

Children particularly move between these stages, dipping in and out of them in what has been called, 'puddle jumping'; one minute they are crying, and the next they are laughing. I have seen this reaction distress bereaved parents, who believe their child is not taking the death seriously, and see this as a sign of irreverence or that they are unaffected by the loss. Neither is true. The child's cognitive development has not yet reached the point where they can distinguish between what is real and unreal. This 'puddle-jumping' is a type of in-built safety mechanism that prevents them being overwhelmed by powerful feelings (Child Bereavement UK). How a child responds to someone dying will be influenced by their age and understanding, the relationship with and attachment they had to the person who died, and how that person died. This will be explored in Chapter 2.

One distressed mother told me that her step-son was running around the garden on the day of his sister's funeral, in the presence of other family mourners, which they found embarrassing and confusing. This boy's mother had died 18 months previously, and it was too hard for him to stay in his grief all the time. This was one way he coped with his feelings of loss.

The lesson here is for adults to learn how NOT to react when a child displays puddle jumping behaviour because this can escalate everyone's distress; instead it would calm everyone down for them to learn how to help the children investigate their grief in language they understand, i.e. metaphorical story. This has the effect of reducing stress, and increasing the attachment bond between adult and child, so that the children feel safe to express their feelings.

The task model of loss

Psychologist J.W. Worden created the Four Tasks of Mourning which can be worked through, focusing on what needs to be accomplished for resolution instead of just being a series of stages through which the bereaved has to pass (Worden, 1991). In this model, the bereaved plays an active rather than a passive role in their grieving process. Worden completed the first long-term study of bereaved children with the Harvard Child Bereavement Study.

The tasks which need to be completed are:

1. To acknowledge and accept the reality of the loss.
2. To **work through** the pain of grief, both physical and emotional.
3. To adjust to life without the deceased.
4. To maintain a connection to the deceased while moving on with life.

Neimeyer criticizes the idea that these tasks, and grief in general, need to be 'worked through'; rather, we need to find meaningful ways of reconstructing meaningful lives. Therapeutic story, with the 'safe distance' of metaphor, helps children to reconstruct meaning after loss and change.

Continuing bonds

According to Phyllis Silverman and Dennis Klass, the bereaved maintains links with the deceased: these bonds are not severed but flow over time (Silverman and Klass, 1996). This model re-examines the view that the purpose of grief is to sever the bonds with the deceased in order to free the survivor to make new attachments. The bereaved actively construct an inner representation of the deceased that is part of the normal grieving process. These continuing bonds are dynamic and developmental. Their research with both adults and children suggests that this is a common experience in people's inner lives, though one that is not always openly shared and publicly acknowledged. Here the grieving process is less about letting go than renegotiating the meaning of the loss over time. While death is permanent and unchanging, the process is not. People are changed by the process; they do not 'get over it'.

They suggest that 'accommodation' is a more appropriate term to use to describe this process. Accommodation suggests a continual activity rather than something which resolves or reaches closure; in the same way as we continually reconstruct ourselves in relation to our social context and our interchanges with others in our lives, so our continuing bonds with the dead person unfold developmentally over time. The past is then incorporated into the whole. The meaning of the dead person in the bereaved person's present life changes continuously.

They argue that we need rituals for continuing bonds with the dead, and where these do not exist formally, we need to creatively reinvent them. This is where ceremonies are helpful on the anniversary of a death. Families I have worked with have created meaningful ceremonies by incorporating elements of their loved ones' interests. For example, an interest in gardening may be utilized by designing a picnic celebration and planting trees in the family member's memory, and then visiting this tree whenever they feel the need to.

In this way the focus on facilitating mourning is on how to 'change connections, to hold the relationship in a new perspective rather than on how to separate, and let go'.

Some children's strategies for maintaining a connection with the deceased are discussed below.

Locating the deceased

The child may need help to understand/talk about where the deceased is at that time, i.e. where the body and soul are. The beliefs of the family are paramount, and many children are confused about the attributes of the dead person in heaven as to whether they can see, hear and move about. A belief in heaven may help the child to maintain a sense that the deceased still exists which may not help them to accept the finality of the death.

I have worked with families whose spiritual framework includes the concept of the after-life, and at the appropriate age, this can be a helpful way for children to start exploring non-Christian concepts.

Experiencing the deceased

Children easily relate to this model, and we see this in the way they describe their lost ones as being 'in heaven', or 'as a star in the sky'; they derive some comfort from being able to continue to communicate with their loved one. Some children will believe that the deceased is watching them, can hear them, or even talk to them. This may be comforting or scary for the child. They may believe that the dead person tries to contact them through dreams. When this happens at school, I believe it is important to remain open to supporting the child's exploration of this subject. One way of supporting them is to encourage them to draw their dreams or write them down. This is something which can be explored in play therapy, so that the child can express their concerns, and help them to develop their spirituality as well as their creative voice. This is an area which I have seen some families fully embrace, and doing so gives the child permission to be open with their parents, and to normalize this part of the grief process. As a child who grew up in a family where relatives talked openly about seeing dead people, I held an early fascination with spirituality, which continues in my life and work.

Reaching out to the deceased

Taking children to the cemetery helps to maintain the connection. I fondly remember visiting the cemetery with my grandmother, to lay flowers on the graves of my great grandparents.

Doing so was not only a bonding experience with my grandmother but a reminder of my ancestors, who they were and how important they were to her. If the loved one has been cremated, it can be helpful for the child to know where their ashes are if they want to look at them.

Talking to the picture of the deceased is another way of maintaining the bonds. Asking questions about the deceased, discussing his/her life with the other members of the family, can help to keep alive the relationship. This discussion can often lead to sharing stories of the deceased which can support the children's grieving process as they remember and reflect on the memories they shared together. This is a great moment where wisdom can be imparted to the next generation.

Waking memories

Thinking about the happy experiences the child had with the deceased usually brings comfort and helps to keep the relationship going. By trying to suppress such thoughts the child may delay the acceptance of the reality of the death. This is a good moment to introduce therapeutic storytelling to children.

Linking objects

Keepsakes or linking objects can help children to have a feeling of the presence of the deceased. Any object which reminds them of the deceased or was given to them by the deceased can be very comforting. Making scrapbooks and memory boxes are often very helpful for children (Cruse Bereavement Care, 2016),

For many cultures, the links the living hold with dead ancestors remain active and are fostered (Barnsley, 1995). Walter (1996) says that the purpose of grief is to learn how to live with the dead, not by learning how to relinquish them, which is the ultimate goal of Western grieving. Walter says it is the other way around with the Shona. They have a simple burial for their dead, not hiding the reality of death, which means that they quickly accept that the person has died physically, and is a 'necessary preliminary to the long-term welcoming of the deceased back as one of the ancestors. The dead person is lost and then re-found, rather than clung onto before being ultimately relinquished.'

This model is not about pretending that the dead person is still alive, nor is it about moving on without those who have died; it's about finding a secure place for them in our narrative and life, where we can relate to them. Helping young children to do this through therapeutic story enables them to find that secure place both internally and externally, and to ease that sense of loss that comes through losing an attachment figure, be it a person, an animal or a home.

The dual process model

This model was developed in the 1990s by Margaret Stroebe and Hank Schut in response to what they argued were the shortcomings of what they described as the traditional 'grief work hypothesis' (Stroebe and Schut, 1999). This provides a perspective for looking at the grief processes in different cultural and ethnic groups, which most 'grief-work' focused hypotheses cannot always do.

This is not a model of symptoms or of problems, positives and negatives, but a map of all the elements involved in the coping process.

They identified two tasks associated with bereavement:

1. *Loss-orientated activities* and stressors directly related to the death. These include crying, yearning, experiencing sadness, denial or anger, dwelling on the circumstances of the death, and avoiding restoration activities.
2. *Restoration-orientated activities* and stressors associated with secondary losses with regard to lifestyle, routine and relationships. These include adapting to a new role, managing changes, developing new ways of connecting with family and friends, and cultivating a new way of life.

Stroebe and Schut suggest that people will invariably oscillate between the two tasks because they need to take respite from dealing with either of these stressors.

Children will be able to identify with both activities when they read the stories in this book with you. It's important to note that these activities do not always occur in a linear fashion. For example, a child may adjust to a loss by developing a connection with family and friends only to encounter more feelings of loss. This shouldn't be interpreted as a setback. Parents often say this to me when their child cries – 'but he was doing so much better!' He probably is because he is learning that crying is a natural part of his grieving process, and eventually he will stop crying and move on to his next task. The characters in the stories learn this lesson, to incorporate the feelings of loss as a natural stage rather than as a setback.

The implications of the Dual Process Model for intervention by practitioners are:

- To recognize the need to pay attention to both dimensions of loss and restoration.
- To recognize the need to both avoid and approach these dimensions/stages.
- To see the 'support of grief work as partial and an incomplete goal for intervention'. There is a need not only to attend to the loss but to pay attention to the secondary changes that have occurred as a consequence of the loss, which are often a significant source of stress.
- To acknowledge the need to take time off from either coping task.

The authors argue that gender differences in response to bereavement suggest that men tend to be restoration-orientated, whilst women are more often loss-orientated in that they are more expressive of their grief. I am careful not to draw on this bias in my practice, because I have seen boys willing to engage in deep emotionally focused therapeutic interventions, and girls wanting a problem-orientated intervention.

This model is particularly relevant to bereaved children who oscillate from loss orientation to restoration orientation – puddle jumping through their grief.

I have seen children often seeking a distraction (restoration orientation) activity after talking about their grief, or using some creative grief intervention, and practitioners should be aware of this and of the child needing to do so, and be prepared to offer a break from the loss orientation with another activity or discussion. For example, a child in my practice painted a series of pictures that poured out of him, one after the other in a series of minutes. During their creation he was silent and focused, concentrating on making his paintings. As soon as he'd finished them, he suddenly put down the paintbrush and walked across the room and started banging the drum loudly. This was his way of marking the end of his loss-making activity and the beginning of a new stage.

The meaning making models

Dramatherapy

Alida Gersie (1991) argues that those experiences we did not have with the deceased become part of the 'Work' of grief, which involves speaking the unspoken, acting this out through drama and play. This enables the pain of the loss to be transformed into a larger framework which helps us to feel less alone.

Therapeutic story

This plays a vital role in providing space and a format for those feelings to be expressed and processed. Children find it easy to relate to their feelings through metaphor, and will identify with story characters who have struggled with similar feelings to their own. By finding themselves in familiar territory in the story, children learn how to cope as the character has. This is the first step towards children building inner resilience; they discover their own strengths, and learn how to locate resources to solve their problems, as their story characters have.

When I read *Isaac and the Red Jumper* with children – a story about a boy who loses his best friend – it prompts children to think about the people in their life who help them cope and they will spontaneously mention their names. I love it when this happens because it tells me that they are remembering people who they can turn to when their feelings overwhelm them. It reminds them that they are not alone in their grief.

Signposting grieving children in the classroom and how to support them

These are the behavioural and emotional signposts that teachers and social workers need to be aware of to identify grieving children in the classroom and prevent them from becoming isolated or excluded.

The regressive behaviour child

Children experiencing an emotional crisis often will act more childlike, immature and may exhibit separation anxiety when away from their parent. They may need to sleep in their parent's bed or need to be held more often than they had previously. It is important to be tolerant of their regressive behaviour at school. Grieving children should not be shamed or told to 'grow up'. These are signals for offering a creative intervention.

The emotional 'numbing' child

Many children in crisis will seem detached from their feelings. It helps them manage their pain. However, behaviourally they will look like they are doing fine because they are not crying and showing their emotions. This does not mean that they are doing fine. As a result, many adults in their life will not check in with them as frequently and they will not get as much support as they may need. This is a sign for a one-to-one.

The acting-out child

An increase in problem behaviour, erratic or explosive emotions, difficulty in concentrating and work-avoidance are all symptomatic of grief. Children may feel helpless, angry, scared, anxious or frustrated. They may be seeking to increase control over their immediate environment because they feel so powerless over their circumstances. These are signs for making a referral for play therapy where the child will play out their feelings and learn how to manage them.

Seven things teachers can do in the classroom

- Tell children the truth when a grieving child is absent from school in the days after the death, with the family's permission.
- Lead a classroom discussion about death and dying and encourage children to express their thoughts and feelings with their peers.
- Dispel rumours: sometimes what a child imagines happened can be worse than the actual reality.
- Create an atmosphere of permission – including tears.
- Be flexible – create time in the curriculum for brief periods of downtime.
- Suggest ways children can cope with and express their feelings after school.
- Offer breaks – if a child is struggling to focus and complete their work, offer them a short break to speak to you.

Toolkit

One of the most useful tools that I use during training professionals is called a '**drawing check-in**'. Teachers, social workers and practitioners have learned to incorporate this tool into their professional practice because it is a way for them to reflect on their feelings. The exercise also helps them to reduce stress and anxiety because creating the drawing connects them to their right brain, where their emotions and feelings are. The drawing itself functions as a container – you literally draw out your feelings onto the page and voilà, you will feel immediately lighter, ready to start your day.

This exercise is best done in the morning, before going to school, which will help you start the day feeling connected to yourself.

All you need to do this exercise is a small Tupperware box filled with coloured crayons and some white A4 paper. I like to include different textures of crayons so that if I feel like scrawling or making heavy marks on the page, I will select the oil pastels which work better than a light pencil.

Set aside 30 minutes to complete this exercise. With practice you will be able to do this in 15 minutes. It is a great way to start the day. Sit somewhere quiet where you will not be disturbed. Turn your phone off. Ask yourself: how am I feeling right now? Select your crayons and draw a picture which represents your feeling. Try not to critique yourself; you aren't creating perfection, just a picture of how you feel. Remember, whatever you produce is OK, it's a reflection of how you feel. When you've finished drawing your picture, take a few moments to look at and reflect on this, and write one word on the drawing which describes your feeling. You are literally meeting yourself on the page, so whatever shows up, just acknowledge it. You will be amazed how powerful this exercise is over time. You can keep the drawings, if you want to or equally, it's fine if you want to immediately dispose of them.

If you want to particularize this exercise and make it about loss, please refer to the exercise in Chapter 3.

Conclusion

When we dare to mention the elephant in the room, we reduce the fantasies that other people may create about this and create an opportunity to learn and grow from the sharing. This equally applies to working with grieving children in the classroom. The more we can learn how to create a safe environment for the grieving children to talk about their feelings of loss and change, the less likely they are to feel overwhelmed by the changes that loss bring and, the more confident they will be.

Chapter 2

Change

The soul wants imaginative responses that move it, delight it, deepen it.

James Hillman, *Inter Views*

In my work with families I see two types of change. Enforced change occurs when children sustain a loss and they have to adjust to the absence of a person or a possession from their lives. The children do not have a choice in these losses: death of a loved one, a friend leaving their school, parents divorcing, losing a pet. Transformative change occurs when the children start to express their feelings about their losses and to make sense of the changes this brings through a creative medium like storytelling. This process needs to be facilitated by an adult who engages with the children not just through the reading of the story but also through the quality of their listening and reflection. By actively listening and reflecting the adult learns where the child is struggling and what they need help with and can then make suggestions for support. So how does change begin?

Although all children (or people, really) may have to endure enforced changes transformative change only occurs when the child is supported and willing to do the work. This process is critical for healthy development and well-being, but without the right support it won't happen … this is why this work is critical, because without the transformative change children will suffer and continue to suffer. This meaning-making process helps them deal with their grief and alleviates suffering.

Have you noticed how children react if you ask them directly 'How do you feel about Granny dying?' Most likely they will look away from you, change the subject, or just shrug and say 'Don't know'. These are typical reactions from children whose cognitive capacity has not yet developed to the stage where they can understand and verbally articulate their feelings, like adults.

The risk, therefore, is that children will feel isolated and lost in their grief if no one is speaking in their language. Children's natural language is play, and they relate more directly to metaphor, which is why we need to consider introducing a different approach to childhood loss and bereavement, if children are to feel heard in their grief.

Therapeutic storytelling is one such approach, which uses metaphor to help bring about healing change in traumatic circumstances such as loss and bereavement. Therapeutic stories create sufficient coherence to facilitate talk about felt confusion or misunderstanding (Gersie, 1997).

The process is powerful in its simplicity. When children identify with the story character (for example, an animal losing his mother), and go on the journey with the character, the children are able to process their traumatic emotions and feelings through the story character.

As a result of this, disturbed thoughts and feelings can be clarified with greater ease, and troubling memories are often worked through in a non-confrontational way for the children. This narrative cover gives children the chance to have their say about their loss without the challenge of committing themselves to an opinion.

The narrative structure of therapeutic stories closely follows the hero's journey, where the main character faces a challenge that he must learn how to overcome. Obstacles will appear along the way, and it's this central challenge which the child can relate to.

The story character learns life lessons, and importantly how to draw on his own inner resources, and those of the helpers who appear on his journey path. The story ends with the character winning his battle, and thus being transformed by the experience.

Rather than having a child read therapeutic stories alone, ideally, therapeutic stories should be read to a child, so that an adult can answer any questions. It's important to recognize that if handled sensitively, a child's questions can lead to them opening up about their circumstances, but this must not be pushed.

Continuing with the animal example, I have heard children express sadness about an animal's loss, which is their indirect way of expressing their own sadness. They feel safe doing this, which means that the grieving process can begin on their terms.

What is therapeutic storytelling?

Stories use metaphor and imagery, a child's natural language for feeling (Sunderland, 2003, p. 2), to change the way we see our lives, and the world. Therapeutic stories connect us to ourselves, and each other, and help us find meaning, hope and resolution for life's problems.

Cantor (2007) defines therapeutic storytelling as 'the process of constructing, co-constructing or otherwise utilising a narrative or anecdote with a client in the interest of achieving a therapeutic goal'.

A well-chosen therapeutic story can become a vital part of a child's healthy, emotional digestive system (Sunderland, 2003, p. xi) by getting to the heart of the matter, and giving children a 'safe distance' through metaphor to deal with their feelings. Readers or listeners project their own motives and emotions onto the characters featured in the story, be they human, animal, tree or a supernatural (imaginary) being. Catharsis and insight will complete the therapeutic impact of the story. The consequence of this healing process is a diminished anxiety, and increased self-esteem (Ayalon in Gersie, 1992, p. 17).

How therapeutic storytelling fits into play therapy

Therapeutic storytelling is one medium in the Play Therapy toolkit, which also includes clay, paint, drawing, music, puppets, drama, movement, role play and sand. Therapeutic storytelling can be used in a non-directive way (the child chooses a story), and a directive way (the therapist selects, or makes up a story in response to the child's needs). The non-directive approach is based on the person-centred model of Carl Rogers and Virginia Axline. In the directive psychodynamic approach, the play therapist directs the child through the creation of a therapeutic story narrative using metaphors from within the child's symptomatology (Joyce Mills), and creative tasks to evoke responses (Alida Gersie).

There are several therapeutic story frameworks used in play therapy, the most common of which is the hero's journey. All frameworks have a beginning, middle and end which enable children to learn and reflect upon their choices and intentions, practise and work out their own understanding and resolution. During their sessions, the children may return to the same story several times until they have played out their internal struggles and reached a resolution that makes sense to them. Through listening, and sometimes dramatizing the story, the children go on an emotional journey which results in a positive effect on their psychological and physical health (Greenberg and Stone, 1992, in Gersie, 1997, p. 14). This encounter enables them to face down their fears, slay their demons within the safety of the story's metaphor, and emerge victorious with new insights about inner resources. The play therapist listens and reflects back the children's experience, thereby strengthening their resolve. The teacher can learn to listen in the same way.

The hero's journey was identified by the American scholar Joseph Campbell. This is a pattern of narrative that appears in drama, storytelling, myth, religious ritual, and psychological development. It describes the typical adventure of the archetype known as The Hero, the person who goes out and achieves great deeds on behalf of the group, tribe, or civilization. Sunderland (2003, p. 23) recommends play therapists use the hero's journey format when making up a therapeutic story:

- identify the child's emotional problem;
- think of characters, a place, and a situation that can provide a metaphorical context for this problem;
- present the main character as grappling with the same emotional problem;
- show the character's main coping strategies which are similar to the child's, and show the failure of these coping mechanisms which results in reaching an internal/external crisis;
- show the journey from the crisis to the solution of the crisis over a bridge between the two;
- show someone or something appearing in the story that helps the character shift, and change direction, and move onto a better coping mechanism.

Historically, therapeutic storytelling has not centralized the spiritual awakening of the character. The focus has been on change occurring when the hero meets another character who introduces the hero to wisdom. In my stories, I have chosen to centralize the spiritual awakening of the hero, which means that sometimes the character's awakening comes from within the hero himself. This comes to him in the form of a dream, visualization or an intuition.

I have chosen this path because the children in my Early Years practice have shown me how attuned they can be to their dreams and intuitions, and how fruitful this attunement is when it is accessed through the creative arts of playing, drawing and storytelling. Once the child has moved through Projective and Sensory Play, to the symbolic stage, which according to Jennings (1999, p. 57) can only happen with the development of the imagination, the child has the capacity to intuitively recognize the authenticity of spiritual truths. When they state these truths directly and out loud, it is with a sense of triumph! The impact and resonance is profound. For example, hearing a child say, 'My frog is the King of his Castle!' is a statement of achievement, empowerment and internal recognition for the child of his or her inner resourcefulness.

Crucial to the creation of a therapeutic story is the capacity for the play therapist and teacher to be able to connect with their own inner child. As Jung discovered, 'through the inner child, opposite qualities within the personality are synthesised and new possibilities are freed' (Jung, 1958, pp. 125–112). To lead others through a story with intimacy and distance, storytellers need to have lived the story from within themselves, and had the experience of the journey (Simms, 2015, Online). Connecting with our own inner child gives us access to our unconscious material, and 'anticipates the figure that comes from the synthesis of conscious and unconscious elements in the personality. It is a unifying symbol that unites the opposites' (Mills and Crowley, 2001, p. 34). The more professionals sit with their story during the quiet time with the children, the more the children unconsciously recognizes the door being opened for them.

The value of therapeutic story

Image and metaphor are the natural language of children (Sunderland, 2003, p. 2). To help children to understand their world, we need to talk their language. Therapeutic story is the key to that language. Therapeutic story offers a child hope of being understood because the story touches the deeper truth of their situation.

In Sunderland's book *A Pea Called Mildred*, Mildred is a pea with dreams. She has great plans for her pea life. However, people are always telling her that dreams are pointless as she is just another ordinary pea. Eventually, with the help of a kind person along the way, Mildred ends up doing exactly what she has always dreamed of doing, and opens a tea shop. In the real world, we perceive a pea as just a pea. Yet in the world of fantasy and metaphor, the pea becomes a symbol that can inspire children to dream. Using metaphor allows the children to enter into the realm of their imagination where anything becomes possible.

Neurological theory supports this idea. Our left-brain hemisphere is analytical, logical, and linear. Our right-brain hemisphere is 'highly specialized to manage complex relationships, patterns, configurations and structures' (Guillaume, 1995, online). While our left brain would tell us the grass was green, our right-brain would focus on the details and deeper meanings. We integrate both ways of processing information to help us navigate in our daily lives. Metaphor speaks directly to the right-brain of the children in language they can understand, and helps them to reframe their reality.

Tyrell (2013, http://www.uncommon-knowledge.co.uk) claims the right story at the right time can facilitate psychological and even physical healing because children can gain access to problem solving solutions, recognize themselves, and learn how to live and function within their world. This is why in non-directed therapeutic play we wait for the children to tell us when that right time is.

In dreams, image and metaphor are the mind's chosen way of processing powerful feelings, so a story is like having a dream while being awake (Sunderland, 2003, p. 5). If the client talks about their dreams in therapeutic play, it's important to listen for the images and symbols they may use as these can give therapists an insight into how to help the child.

A child who has experienced a recent loss may have nightmares and teaching staff may hear about these, particularly if they are vivid and/or disturbing. This is where using active listening is particularly helpful. If you notice children are talking about their dreams or nightmares, take them aside into a quiet space where you can invite them to tell you about some of the detail. I recommend using a discussion prompt, such as making a dreamcatcher. However, if you don't feel comfortable doing this, talk to the parent first and your SEN about your concerns. Consider making a referral to a counsellor or play therapist. In preparation for making any referral, I recommend completing the assessment tool called Strengths and Difficulties Questionnaire by Goodman. This will tell you where on the spectrum of needs the child sits.

The children can then take the dreamcatcher home with them. Nightmares can make children feel discombobulated and making this object gives the children a sense of containment which can lead to empowerment. Below are some examples of dreamcatchers I made with the children at Great Ormond Street Hospital for Children.

These are simple and can be made in 15 minutes. At the Craft Station in Outpatients, my team and I never knew how long we would have a child sitting with us before the doctor called them in for their appointment. Sometimes the child sat crafting for just 15 minutes, but that was enough time to make a dreamcatcher. The key was having the 'ingredients' ready to make them. When the children returned to the hospital the following week for further tests or treatment, the parents would tell us how helpful the dreamcatcher had been for the children in terms of easing their anxiety. So, assemble the following items into a small, mobile, hand carrying container:

- Coloured card and tissue paper
- Glue
- Pipe cleaners
- Scissors
- Felt tip pens.

Explain to the children the purpose of the dreamcatcher, which is to catch bad dreams. Invite the children to draw a circle and cut this out. Invite them to decorate this. Ask them to choose some coloured paper and cut this into strips for them. This direct action not only saves time but also helps the children to feel supported and nurtured. Finish off the dreamcatcher by sticking a pipe cleaner to the top so that this can either be pinned or stuck to the bedhead or, side table, wherever the children want to keep it. Congratulate them on making this dreamcatcher and invite them to tell you about their experience of it. Keep this part light because they may not want to, but at least you have given them the opportunity to circle back to you.

Making dreamcatchers can be expanded into a small group or class activity where children learn about how their brains benefit from having this small container to hold their anxieties and worries.

During this exercise, notice the language the child uses to describe his or her nightmare and dreams. Talking indirectly to children through metaphor helps them to feel safe and willing to access their feelings about a problem they are unable to talk about. Mills and Crowley (1986, p. 50) believe that 'all presenting problems and symptoms are really metaphors that contain a story about what the problem really is'. In this way the metaphor is the message, and contains the solution for the child's problem. Ask yourself if there is anything in the child's discussion of his or her dream/nightmare which contains a possible solution. By starting the discussion with this intention in mind, you will be actively listening and more likely to hear something which you can repeat back to the child.

Sunderland (2003, p. 38) argues that rather than expressing the problem directly which would shame and embarrass the child, professionals must use language of imagining rather than the everyday language of thinking to engage the child. This method also allows the professional to convey the depth and colour and richness of the child's feelings, which is why therapeutic story is such a valuable tool in the therapeutic play tool kit.

Therapeutic stories give children access to difficult and traumatic feelings so that they can process them in language they understand, without feeling threatened. The

professional is with them to support them and give them a safe space in which to process their feelings through the story, and to listen to and respond to their reactions, and body language.

Elements of therapeutic story

The hero's journey

To construct a successful therapeutic story using the hero's journey, we need to create a structure from crisis through to resolution. The key stops along the way are highlighting the hero's journey of struggle and reconciliation as they learn to reframe their reality through the metaphor.

All the stories contained in this book have been designed with the hero's journey in place, so they are ready for you to use.

Symptomatology

Erickson pioneered an approach of 'utilization' whereby patients' presenting symptoms were accepted and incorporated into the treatment strategy (Mills and Crowley, 1986, p. 45). In this way therapists are working with what the client presents. The therapist must create the therapeutic metaphor out of the conscious and unconscious information the client presents.

I used this format successfully with the children in outpatients at Great Ormond Street Hospital for Children who were anxious about their appointments and procedures. However, time was a factor, as we never knew how long we had with them at the Craft Station before they were called for their appointment. This reminds me of the situations teaching staff face all the time during the school day; children may share something significant just as the bell rings or, while standing in line at the lunch queue, or after detention. There are myriad of opportunities. So, at GOSH, I found a way of adapting the therapeutic story format so that it could be done quickly, on a single sheet of A4 paper.

The children loved this method because it was visual and quick. Their attention was often diverted by hospital noises, and having a single page to draw them back to helped me to keep their attention focused.

I was aware of the work of Professor Mooli Lahad, an educational psychologist and director of the MA studies in Dramatherapy at Tel Hai College, Israel. He created the BASIC Ph model of coping and resiliency in the wake of both natural and man-made disasters. He worked closely with Alida Gersie on her Six Part Story-Making method (6PSM). This is a creative format of making up stories and exploring their dramatic and therapeutic potential for individuals and groups (Shacham and Lahad, 2012, p. 47). Lahad and Gersie noticed during their five-year collaboration that the invented stories were revealing the students' ways of coping which corresponded with Lahad's model of resiliency.

After completing training in 6PSM, I decided to introduce the 6PSM to outpatients at GOSH. The results were astonishing and can be applied in the school environment too. I did, however, make some adaptations of my own to 6PSM, to tailor it for the hospital environment.

I particularly liked 6PSM because stories told in 6PSM are based on a hero-quest sequence which is easy to explain to children, given the vast number of comic book heroes now available on film! The moment you mention the word 'hero' or 'superhero' to children, they get the significance of what you are asking them to imagine, and quickly dive into their collection of stories. Jung and M.L. von Franz (1964), the researcher of fairy tales and stories based on a Jungian approach, found that six questions are always represented in fairy tales, and these are used as the story structure in 6PSM:

1. Who is (are) the main character/s (hero/heroine)?
2. What is the task or mission of the main character/s?
3. Who or what can help (if at all)?
4. What is the obstacle in the way or what prevents it from happening?
5. How does/do the main character/s cope with the obstacle?
6. What happens next or how does the story end?

The way to start using the 6PSM is to get a blank piece of A4 and divide this into six boxes using a coloured pen chosen by the children. By inviting the children to choose the colour you are including them in the process.

Then in each box ask the corresponding question. I ask the question and invite the children to draw their answer in each box. As the story continues and builds the children usually gets completely absorbed in telling it, and their energy and movement changes. This is how you know they are making connections with their own story. When the story is finished, this is your opportunity to reflect on how the children are or are not coping and to help you decide on the intervention possibilities.

Teachers can use this intervention with children which would be a useful assessment tool to use prior to making a therapeutic referral. You may find that completing this tool is enough for the child. Lahad suggests asking yourself the following questions during this reflection:

- Does this story suggest an intervention that is balancing, helping the child to 'bounce back'? Is it about regaining strengths and separating from the teacher after a short and focused encounter?
- Does the story show very few coping resources, or too many channels in conflict? If so, then a longer therapy may be indicated.
- Does the story reveal developmental concerns and conflicts that belong to a very young age or are not at all age appropriate?
- Are the character's problems chronic, or is the quest circular, so that a supportive approach maybe the most suitable recommendation?

Some story examples from the Craft Station at GOSH are below:

All these stories were created within 15–20 minutes and show the children's process of coping with and resolving their conflicts. I believe this is a useful tool for supporting children

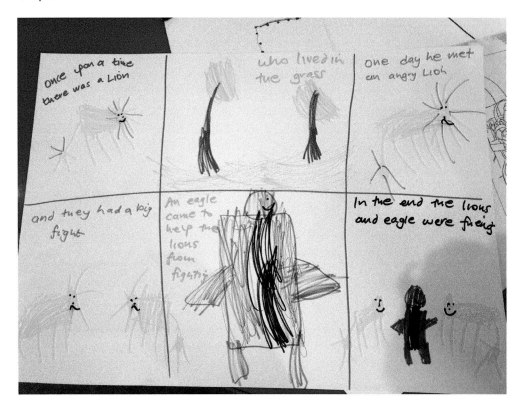

in processing their conflicts and one way of helping children cope with loss and change which could be easily incorporated into the school day. However, if the children struggle to complete this exercise I would consider this as a warning sign for which further intervention should be considered.

Listening to the children's needs

You might be wondering what the criteria are for using therapeutic story. The key is to listen to the children's needs, and to create the story around those. Erickson views symptom as a message or 'gift' (Mills and Crowley, 1986, p. 45) from the unconscious that can be used to resolve the symptom. The heart of Erickson's approach is a philosophy of acceptance and validation of the child's presenting behaviour (Mills and Crowley, 1986, p. 47) which is consistent with Axline's second principle of accepting the child as she or he is. Erickson's technique of utilisation also requires professionals to be skilled in observing, participating in and reframing what the child presents in the clinical situation (Mills and Crowley, 1986, p. 48). For example, if the child has high energy, match that energy by choosing high energy kangaroos or monkeys.

Mellon refers to the 'Four Elements' guidelines that have helped her to create and organize stories. 'If your child is full of fire, and stomps about the house, then you need not waste your time with a story about a little gerbil …' (Mellon, 2000, p. 57). Similarly, children who are more connected with air than fire, who leap lightly about on their toes respond to lilting stories filled with bright birds.

Next we can start to develop a strategy and story framework and put the chosen issues into a metaphorical context to which we know the children will relate. The key here is to choose an idea from a story source we know, either a literary metaphor, fictional metaphor, a fairy tale, a myth or drawn from our own experience. This is where the character we choose as our protagonist will share the same emotional problem – metaphorical conflict as the children. This is where we need to know the emotional themes that recur in the children's play (Sunderland, 2003, p. 23) so that the journey the children will go on through the story will be the same as their own, and they will be able to identify with the character's defeats and obstacles, and ultimately feel the character's triumph.

This is how the empathy gets through to the children (Sunderland, 2003, p. 16). For example, my client had an issue with being the only mixed-race child in the school, and had feelings of not belonging. I chose a fantastical context – a tea pot called Tilly who was born in a pot factory, and who is the only tea pot with a crinkly spout. This provided the protection of disguise and indirect expression for my client which allowed her to explore her feelings through this metaphorical fantasy. It is through fantasy that the child learns to make sense of her outside world (Mills and Crowley, 1986, p. 36). This metaphor helped me to change the literal into the symbolic for my client. As Sunderland says, sometimes the more 'dotty' the better (Sunderland, 2003, p. 25). By creating this metaphor I had also created a three-way empathic relationship between child, therapist and story which made it possible for the child to develop a sense of identification with the characters and events of the metaphor. It is this sense of identification that contains the transformational power of the metaphor (Mills and Crowley, 1986, p. 65) as I witnessed after I had read this story to my client.

As Combs and Freedman state (1990, p. 45), our clients tell us where to look to create metaphors. We learn this by entering our clients' world of thinking, feeling and the unconscious, and by listening and paying attention to what they tell us and how they move and behave and play. And finally we use symbols to gather information about our client's mood and intentions. Professionals in the classroom are in a unique position to catch these stories and to discover story metaphors within them.

In my story, Tilly's crinkly spout symbolized my client's long hair that was beaded in the Afro/Caribbean culture. My client struggled to accept her identity and self-image, and her play reflected that struggle. Each week she could not accept that her dolls' long hair plaits were good enough. After hearing the story about Tilly T. Pot my client reached a point of self-acceptance on this issue that we were able to celebrate.

The next step is to create a multi-dimensional perspective that shows the main character using similar methods (coping strategies) to deal with the problem as those used by the child – personify the unconscious processes in the form of heroes and helpers (representing the protagonist's abilities and resources), and villains and obstructions (representing the protagonist's negative beliefs) (Mills and Crowley, 1986, p. 66).

In my story these qualities were represented by a gang-leader milk jug called Billy who represented Tilly's unconscious and unexpressed powerful voice, and Mr Box who represented Tilly's fear of being excluded from the group. These methods will then lead the protagonist into a metaphorical crisis. This is the crux of the story. In my story, Tilly reached her crisis when she realized that by isolating herself from the crowd of other pots, she had missed seeing that they also had markings that made them look different.

She was able to shift and change direction when Billy the milk jug noticed her distress and spoke up for her. Tilly's parallel learning situation was recognizing that she wasn't really alone. In order to avoid moving the story along too quickly I used a bridge section of a protest staged by the other members of the T. set which enabled Tilly to feel connected to the group. Her new sense of identification as no longer alone and also unique is the result of her successful completion of the hero's journey (Mills and Crowley, 1986, p. 66). The story culminates with the pots celebrating altogether, and by Tilly and everyone else acknowledging Tilly's bravery in speaking up for herself and finding her voice. This was mirrored by my client. Finding her voice was a key theme in her therapeutic play journey.

Metaphor activates unconscious association patterns and response tendencies that give the child's consciousness a new and better way of responding. (Mills and Crowley, 1986 p. 19). Tilly and my client found a different way of responding by going on the hero's journey and finding their inner resources to help them triumph.

Co-evolution

As Bateson says about co-evolution, 'if the therapist is to have any influence on the evolution of the client system, he or she must join sufficiently with that system to function as part of a larger mind that includes both for a while' (Combs and Freedman, 1990, p. 37). In therapeutic play the therapist enters the child's world, and learns what children are saying in their play by not directing them. Likewise, professionals are already within the children's world and are therefore already alongside them.

Using metaphor to facilitate therapeutic processes

The therapeutic story takes the children on a journey with the intention of helping them reframe their perceptual frame through which their problem can symbolize something other than pain and emotional agony. (Combs and Freedman, 1990, p. 66). Teaching professionals are in a unique position of knowing the children and their circumstances, which gives them a window into understanding how to help the children reframe their circumstances.

Benefits of therapeutic storytelling

Ultimately as professionals, we are trying to understand the children better, and help them to understand themselves better too. In the words of the poet Seamus Heaney, a therapeutic story can therefore 'amplify the music of what happens' (Sunderland, 2003, p. 11).

The language of therapeutic storytelling

A therapeutic story is constructed around metaphor using myths, fairy tales, folktales, fantasy, animal lore, science fiction settings, combined with made up stories from the children's imagination, and symptomatology (Mills and Crowley, 2001, p. 40).

The neuroscientific effect of using metaphor

Neuroscience research shows that more brain centres light up in response to metaphor than any other form of human communication forming new neural pathways (F. Levin, 1997 and A.H. Modell, 1997 in Wilkinson, 2006, p. 9). Symbolic/fantasy play with its use of metaphors provides new experiences that develop the brain/mind. This is important evidence for teachers to use when working with therapeutic story.

The origin of oral storytelling traditions

Oral storytelling originated in simple chants, with our ancestors gathered around their fires to express their fears, beliefs and heroism through oral narratives. The hero's tale originated through the creation of myths to explain natural occurrences. This long tradition of storytelling is evident in ancient cultures such as the Australian Aborigines, the African Bushman, and the Native American Shaman. Community storytelling explained how life began and why things happened, as well as providing entertainment. Communities were strengthened through stories that connected the present, the past and the future. Early storytelling combined stories, poetry, music and dance. Those who excelled at storytelling became entertainers, educators, cultural advisers and historians for the community. Through storytellers, the history of a culture was handed down from generation to generation.

In the 1800s Jakob and Wilhelm Grimm collected and edited oral tales, and Peter Christen Asbjørnsen and Jorgen Moe collected Norwegian folk tales. In Denmark Hans Christian Andersen adapted folktales he heard from oral storytellers. In England, Joseph Jacobs recorded collections of folktales of England, Scotland and Wales. Myths and stories from North America, South and Central America, Europe and Near East, Asia, and Africa are still used today in therapeutic storytelling. These folktales, and fairy tales were later analysed by Bruno Bettelheim in *The Uses of Enchantment* (Wikipedia, online), and show how fairy tales are, according to the Jungian analyst M.L. von Franz, the purest and simplest expression of collective unconscious psychic processes. She goes on to argue that the most frequent way archetypal stories originate is through individual experiences. So by using elements of fairy tales and myth, we might be able to see the way that the child self projects itself into reality in order to 'meet' the world (Lahad, p. 48). This is one way professionals can get access to the child's inner world.

Different therapeutic storytelling approaches

Bibliotherapy

The Bibliotherapy approach fits into the person-centred, non-directed play therapy model developed by Virginia Axline and Carl Rogers. While this approach is intended for use by therapists, this would usually be the most successful approach for teachers. In this approach, the therapist chooses a prepared story to read with the children, one that reflects the children's presenting problem. This allows the children to 'walk in the shoes' of another person, and to see themselves from the outside (Cantor, 2007, p. 16). Afterwards, the therapist can lead a discussion with the children about their responses to the story which can help the children gain insight into their life, and situation. Some therapeutic stories (Sunderland's books in particular) use pictures to invoke emotional responses which enable the child to interact with the story, and the therapist.

The mutual storytelling technique

Gardner (1970) was the first individual to develop a structured application of a storytelling technique in psychotherapy with children that was client driven or created. He recognized children enjoyed both telling and listening to stories, and developed The Mutual Storytelling Technique, as a means of utilising storytelling therapeutically, and discovering psychodynamic meaning, drawing on Freudian and Kleinian theory (Mills and Crowley, 1986, p. 42). He believed that a child-created story would contain the elements of the psychodynamic conflicts with which the child was struggling. Gardener used an introduction like 'Good morning boys and girls, I'd like to welcome you once again to Dr Gardner's Make-Up-A-Story Television programme'. Gardner instructed the children to make up a story that a) contained adventure and excitement; b) should not be about a personal experience, or from a TV or movie; c) had a beginning, middle and end; and d) had a moral. The therapist then probed the story for psychodynamic meaning, and created another story using the same characters and setting but introducing 'healthier adaptations' than those described in the child's story.

StoryPlay

Mills and Crowley (1986) moved away from finding psychodynamic meaning to looking at behavioural subtleties actually taking place in the session. She called this method Storyplay which created original metaphors that used a three-level communication process incorporating interspersed suggestions (drawing on Erikson's 'utilisation' approach), and a process of 'sensory interweaving' into an engaging storyline. Mills emphasized the child's sensory preferences as being the key to how they learned, saw their world, and coped with their presenting problem. As sensory play is now well used in schools, this is a useful example of how a child's sensory system can be put to good use using storytelling. Mills used the example of children who were struggling with spelling because their teacher was using a phonetics system whereas the children had a visual sensory system, and needed to see the words rather than hear them. Mills devised a story based on a visual format. Learning a child's sensory preferences then allows the professional to facilitate a therapeutic experience of 'sensory synchronicity' that gives the child access to a rich and accessible 'treasure chest' of inner resources, which can form the basis of the therapeutic story (Mills, 1986, pp. 102–104).

Fairy tales

Bruno Bettelheim (1976), was an Austrian-born writer and Freudian psychologist known for his discussions of the therapeutic use of fairy tales. He was the author of *The Uses of Enchantment*, in which he discussed the meaning and importance of fairy tales, such as those published by the Brothers Grimm. He suggested that if children were allowed to read and interpret fairy tales in their own way, they would gain a greater sense of meaning and understanding about the issues in their lives. (Bettelheim, 1976 in Cantor, 2007).

Therapeutic story-making (TSM)

Alida Gersie (1992) is a drama therapist who has written extensively about the uses of therapeutic story-making with bereaved children. Her story-based method facilitates productive change in seemingly hopeless situations. Therapeutic Story-making (TSM) emphasizes the story as an 'emergent dialogue and performance, and uses the listener's engagement in a speaker's narrative constructions, and facilitates constructive re-narration by means of creative-expressive dialogue-based processes (response tasks)' (Gersie, 1997, pp. 50–51).

Unlike narrative psychology that conceives of stories in terms of monologue, and text, TSM includes the listener in the therapeutic situation, and evocation of the narrative. Gersie selects stories from oral traditions from indigenous cultures, and weaves into the storytelling creative tasks, and exercises that turn readers, and listeners from passive audience to active participants, eliciting their own images, and creating their own myth. Her story-making structures are effective because they take the reader on a personal journey which parallels the story's journey. This makes TSM a dynamic, interactive method which involves both listener and narrator in the story-making process. This method is highly constructed, with the therapist leading the listener through the creative-expressive dialogue-based processes, and providing the framework for the response tasks. For this reason I imagine TSM works well with a group of bereaved children who need a strong framework of support to hold their grief when it feels overwhelming. This framework will also provide encouragement for children to test out their fears within a safe context.

Archetypal psychology

James Hillman (1997), founder of Archetypal Psychology, and Patron of the Sesame Institute since 2006 said that 'enacting a story connects imagination in the body. It does not turn imagination into meaning as psychoanalysis has been doing for the past one hundred years' (Sesame Institute, 2011, Online). Hillman was the first Director of the Jung Institute in Zurich, and critical of 20th century psychologies, saying they were, 'reductive, materialistic, and literal; they are psychologies without psyche, without soul' (Wikipedia). Hillman saw the soul at work in imagination, fantasy, myth and metaphor, the essence of story-making, and storytelling. His approach was dynamic, interactive, and integrative.

The spontaneous story-making method

Nancy Mellon champions a spontaneous story-making method which involves listening to your own inner child as much as the child you are working with, and works frequently with the body's organs, views them each as having a distinctive voice. She believes this allows you to connect with your inner story-making.

Grief work is akin to heroic work, both can be both overwhelming outside a secure frame- work. This is especially true for children who struggle to express their grief verbally. Teachers may see evidence of this struggle in a child's behaviour in the classroom. Grief can be expressed through a child's poor concentration, which can deteriorate when their feelings are overwhelming. Maybe they are thinking about Grandad's funeral or, being unable to say goodbye to their beloved pet. If it's difficult to say these things out loud, the first clue is to look for unusual behaviour: lack of focus, being easily distracted.

I believe bereaved children find their voice through metaphorical story, and I am interested in providing a space where the children's narrative can be understood, and heard. 'Narrative as the therapeutically valued, client expressed story of the self is key to the foundation of psychotherapy. In the context of play therapy, narrative approaches once again look to a form of expression that is not totally reliant upon language.' Landreth (2002, p. 304) reminds us that toys are children's words, and play is their language. Therefore a narrative approach to play therapy can be construed simply as play therapy itself wherein the therapist respects the forms of expression of that narrative that are available to the children through the Play Therapy toolkit. I agree with Cantor (2007, p. 12) that 'narrative therapists seek to re-author the dominant problem-saturated stories in a client's life'. The study of therapeutic storytelling illuminates that for many clinical approaches, both classic and mode. Storytelling frequently involves the creation of a new story. It's the new story that I am interested in helping bereaved children find. The teacher has a unique role to be able to catch these stories and help bereaved children re-create their story.

Why therapeutic storytelling helps with grief processes

In the classroom, teachers can use these stories to help children to work through these stages, express their grief, and learn how to accept their loss. Gersie (1992, p. 38) argues that the questions children ask about death (which depend on their stage of development) are compelling because they lead to questions about life: who are we, why are we here, and how can we live in accordance with what we know. These questions can be explored richly through TSM, because life and death represent the opening and closing of story.

Case examples of how I have used therapeutic storytelling

Bibliotherapy

I have read therapeutic stories to bereaved children during play therapy sessions, and used that as a basis for starting a dialogue with them, either through talking, or using an artistic metaphor through drawing. I have used the book *Isaac and the Red Jumper* (Seyderhelm, 2013) which follows the hero's journey format, which has enabled the children to identify with the character, and go on their own journey through the story, arriving at their own conclusions about loss, death and life.

As you use these stories in the classroom, by inviting the children to draw in response to the story, you are focusing on integrating left- and right-brain functions on a conscious and unconscious level. This helps to expand the metaphorical message into tangible, and personal terms for the children through imagery, colours and shapes. For example, I heard one child say that reading the book helped him realize that you shouldn't just live in a world of grey and black, a 'colour-ending' world forever and ever, and that even when you died, you could live on in a colourful world. I have heard children express sadness about an animal's loss, which is their indirect way of expressing their own sadness. They feel safe doing this, which means that the grieving process can begin on their terms.

Therapeutic story-making (TSM)

I have developed my therapeutic storytelling practice with several groups of clinicians counselling bereaved children using Gersie's TSM, to engage and re-story. I read the story (*Hemi and the Whale* by Ronald Leonard Bacon) to them as a way of evoking their unconscious, and igniting their imagination before asking them to draw a picture in response to the story. In this way they were creating their own 'story within a story'.

Teacher's Toolkit

The importance of the teacher/child relationship in therapeutic story

Next to parents and caregivers, a teacher is usually the most significant other in a young child's life, with the power to influence and engage that child, to help him or her grow and develop, build courage and resilience. All of this is done as well as engaging within the context of the educational task (P. Salmon, 1995, *Psychology in the Classroom*, London: Cassell).

Developmental psychology shows us that the child's self-image is internalized from significant others. The teacher's ability to listen actively, respond empathically, provide consistency and establish clear boundaries can all help the child feel secure within this relationship. You help the child develop a more positive sense of self by showing that both his anxieties and his story have been, as D. Winnicott (1960, *The Maturational Processes and the Facilitating Environment*, London: Hogarth Press, p. 240) puts it, 'held in mind'. This holding in mind needs to be made explicit to the pupil and it is the practical ways of doing this that underpin my therapeutic storytelling approach.

For example, by using active listening skills the teacher can show the children she is aware of their personal anxieties. Reflective comments made verbally or in writing on the children's work are used to show the children that the feelings expressed in their story have been thought about. With the security the children receive from knowing the teacher has held them in mind, they becomes less preoccupied with their anxieties and are able to focus on the educational task (Waters, 2004).

How to use these stories

These stories are intended for use by professionals in primary schools. They are short enough to be read through in 15 minutes, and the questions at the end of the story can be worked through with the child. You will need to set aside half an hour to complete these questions with the creative exercises. I recommend that these are done in a safe space where the child can access creative materials and be quiet.

When should I use a therapeutic story?

If you notice that children are stuck or having difficulty expressing their feelings, that is the time to suggest reading a story with them. I emphasize with and not to – the difference is subtle and important when suggesting this to children. By using the word with instead of to, you are telling children that you are participating in this act together; this is not a teacher/ pupil situation where there is an obvious power difference between those roles. In reading therapeutic stories with children you are starting a process where you are their companion, you do not have the answers to how they will respond to this story, and so in this way you aren't teaching them anything. They are in fact teaching you by allowing you to enter their inner world through metaphor. This is what gives them the safe distance to be able to open up to you.

A word about empathy

Empathy is your most important tool for you to use when reading a therapeutic story with children, and by constructing an empathic response you constantly give the children permission to tell their story. See Chapter 3 for more about empathy.

One of the most powerful benefits of using therapeutic storytelling is giving the children a context in which to explore their 'anti-social' behaviour so that they no longer need to act this out in the classroom. When they discover their demons and monsters in a story, this is where they can leave them.

The one rule

One reason why therapeutic approaches are not used in primary schools is the legitimate concern around being able to maintain confidentiality and relationship boundaries. By staying in the metaphor when reading a therapeutic story to a child, and only expressing interpretations within the metaphor of the story, you minimize these concerns (Waters, *Therapeutic Storywriting*, p. 19). Remember, the metaphor functions as the children's emotional cover, so stay in it until they are ready to come out of it. If you come out of the metaphor and start discussing the children's feelings, they may simply shut down. You will know when children are ready to abandon the metaphor when they start talking directly about their feelings. An example of metaphorical language is 'the tortoise feels sad about not seeing the ducks today'; the children are talking through the metaphor, whereas if they wanted to speak directly about their feelings they might say, 'I feel sad about not seeing my friend Freddie today.' In either version, take your cue from the children. Don't rush them to come out of the metaphor, they will tell you when they are ready to do so, and meanwhile, use this as an opportunity to learn more about what's upsetting them.

How to follow up and reflect back to the child

One of my clients chose to construct his own story through drawing pictures. This began when I asked him to draw me a tree, a house and a person, a useful exercise to use if a child is stuck in his emotional process. This child was very stuck, so much so that talking was impossible for him, he uttered single words, and his eye contact with me was non-existent.

He looked down at the floor most of the time, with his head falling almost onto his chest. He was distressed but he could not verbally tell me why. However, when he began to draw the tree, I noticed that his body language and posture changed; he sat up straighter, and drew his picture with some attention and consideration. Afterwards, during our discussion about the tree, I asked him to tell me more about the roots of his tree.

'Those aren't roots, those are tunnels,' he said.

'Ah, those are tunnels,' I said, curiously and empathically. I had wrongly assumed they were roots, which just goes to show – never assume what a child's drawing means! Let the child explain, if he wants to.

'Yes, the tunnels are for the moles,' he said.

I was intrigued, and as I continued to ask him open questions and empathize with his answers, so he began to tell me the story of the mole family. This story continued over several sessions, until he had extended his drawing over several pages of A4, and stuck these pages together. The mole story was told entirely through metaphor; at no point did he come out of this and talk about his feelings, which told me that he was not yet ready to make any comparisons between the mole family and his own, but there were some very interesting aspects in the story which told me something about how he was struggling with feeling lost and alone since his grandad had died.

Symptoms of grieving and the accompanying stories

This book focuses on grief and healing in general and in different situations; for murder, suicide and death through war and natural disasters, reactions may be different, and I refer you to consult specialist support for these areas.

Changes in behaviour

At times children may seem unaffected by the death and play happily as if nothing has happened. But watch out for any changes in their behaviour, which could be their way of expressing feelings they can't talk about. These could include:

- Clinginess. Refusing to be left or clinging to you or someone else can be how children express the need for reassurance that important people aren't going to die and leave them too.
- Distance. Some children can put up a barrier with remaining members of the family because they're scared of getting hurt again. They might want to spend more time away from home, with friends or at school.
- Aggression. This may be your child's way of expressing helplessness in the face of loss.
- Regression. How children respond to death can vary a lot from day to day. Acting like a younger child can be a sign of insecurity. Young children may start wetting or soiling themselves, or want a long-forgotten bottle or dummy. They may become more prone to illness or even lose weight.
- Lack of concentration. Your child may find it hard to concentrate at school and fall behind with in work.
- Sleep problems. Your child may find it hard to sleep and become afraid of the dark.

The therapeutic stories that follow deal with the symptoms of loss and contain creative tools to help children express their feelings and build resilience:

- **Aggression** after a teacher leaves primary school
- **Anger** after the death of a friend
- **Anxiety** after the death of a pet
- **Clinginess** after the death of a parent
- **Feeling different** after being adopted
- **Magical thinking** after the death of a sibling
- **Separation anxiety** after the loss of a friend
- **Separation anxiety** after parents' divorce
- **Sleep disruptions** after the death of a grandparent.

This kind of work does trigger adult losses, and one of my key messages is to help adults learn how to separate their own feelings of loss from those of the children they are reading with, which makes adults more effective – a clearer channel for the work – look at Chapter 3 for some case examples of adults struggling and how they coped, or anecdotes about how adults have dealt with being the caregiver and also having to grieve on their own.

At the end of each story there are two options for the teacher to choose from depending on how much time he/she has:

- The main course exercise – to be done out of classroom – 121 and in groups – 30 minutes.
- The appetizer – adapted for the classroom – can be done in 10–15 minutes.

The deck of cards

You can download a set of cards from my website. Each card has a key message written on one side and is blank on the other side for children to write or draw on after the exercise, to record their thoughts/feelings.

Classroom activity

There are two exercises at the end of each story, the Appetizer and the Main Course. These have been designed to give you choices in the classroom depending on the scale of the issue the child presents and, the amount of time you have available at the time to deal with this issue. Think of them as your 'go to' classroom tools. When the emotional temperature suddenly heats up and looks like it may be about to boil over, use one of these exercises to try and bring the temperature down. Remember this type of overheated response happens when the children's invisible (emotional) backpack starts to feel too heavy for them to carry anymore, which is why their reaction is to have a meltdown. At that point they have moved out of the left side of their rational brain and are in the fight or flight side with their feelings. This is where using creative tools can reach them and help them to recalibrate their emotional response.

These exercises are meant to be used interchangeably and repeated as often as is necessary. The point you are aiming for is for the children to learn how to contain their feelings and express their needs without needing an external trigger. If you find after completing these exercises a few times that the children are still distressed and acting out, it is possible that the issue is more deeply rooted in the children's psyche and possibly influenced by their family dynamic. At this point I would recommend a more direct therapeutic intervention, like play therapy, where the issue can be addressed over a period of time with a qualified therapist who can hold these difficult situations and offer support to the family.

You will find these exercises at the end of each story. In preparation and before using these exercises, I recommend that you gather together the creative resources I have used into a box and keep this box in your classroom. That way you can easily access this when the situation arises. Make sure that when you have used a resource that you replace it because I guarantee that if you don't, that will be the one resource you need! Save yourself the energy and hassle of looking for this resource when your attention and focus needs to be with the children. They may ratchet up the volume if they see you unprepared which may then have a knock-on effect on your stress levels.

Appetizer

Each story in this book has a different Appetizer which is unique to that story's context. This is a 10-minute exercise designed to contain the children's emotions quickly so that they can remain in the classroom and continue with their work. If you find that the children do not settle after doing this exercise then move onto the Main Course. Tell the children you will schedule the 30 minutes required to complete the Main Course and prepare yourself following the instructions below. Tell them when the Main Course exercise will take place.

Main course no. 1: Four-part pizza

This is a 30-minute exercise designed to satisfy the children's immediate emotional need and help them to formulate and articulate their request for change and help. What tends to happen is that the children's request often gets drowned out by the volume of their emotional distress, so these questions are designed to help them uncover those requests. This exercise is based on Marshall Rosenberg's NVC method and contains four key questions. I have adapted these and made them child-friendly, so instead of simply asking the children the questions, you are going to invite them to make a 'pizza on paper' by answering one question per slice. They get to decorate each slice with different toppings, which you are going provide in the form of crafts. This four-part pizza Main Course will be the same for each story. My reason for this is it provides a clear framework for you to contain the children within while being playful enough for them to engage with. Afterwards you will be able to use this information to assess their progress, and may find that they want to return to it and make another pizza on paper!

Pizza ingredients

Below is an example of the four-part pizza main course exercise. Blank sheets of this are available at the back of the book for you to photocopy and give to the children to fill out.

Start by having a set of crayons available as well as glue and coloured tissue paper for this exercise.

The children will have witnessed something or, engaged in an exchange which has triggered their emotional response. You are going to use this as the focus for this exercise so you can understand what unmet emotional need is driving this response. Be prepared for anything! Try to set aside any judgement or preconceptions you may have about this child and stay open. This will help you to attune your listening and hear what they are telling you which will in turn make them feel heard.

Give them the blank pizza on paper and explain that there are four slices to the pizza. Each slice has a different topic and you want them to draw their response in each slice and then give one word for each slice. They are free to choose whichever resource they want from your box. Explain that the tissue paper can be folded or torn and stuck onto the pizza. The one rule is that they have to keep their drawings inside the lines of the pizza slices. This is to help them start to contain their feelings and responses as they go through this exercise.

The four slices

You say:

1. When I see, hear, remember, imagine (name the triggering incident)
2. I feel emotion, sensation – (name that emotion or sensation)
3. Because I need SOMETHING – (what is it that you need?)
4. Would you be willing to do X for me (their request)?

For example:

1. **When I** hear someone talking about their grandma
2. **I feel** angry
3. **Because I** want to talk to my grandma but can't because she's dead
4. **Would you be willing** to talk to me about my grandma?

In this example, the children need to be heard, to have their grief and loss acknowledged.

Child: 4 part PIZZA

Main course no. 2: Unpacking your backpack

We all carry an invisible backpack around with us on our life journey. In the backpack we carry our story. This consists of our hopes and dreams, fears, anxieties, losses, life's experiences and expectations, and these influence and shape our identity and sense of self, who we are, what we do, and how we go about our daily life. The story contents of our backpack affect the way we think, feel and act: towards ourselves, towards others, and towards our life generally.

When these build up and up until the backpack is overflowing, that is when we can be triggered to react in an inappropriate way. Children who are dealing with some form of loss usually carry heavy backpacks, so one of the most useful tools you can include in your toolkit is teaching them about how to empty their backpacks so that they can contain the good stuff.

My aim in helping them to unpack the backpack is to allow them to *express* and *explore* feelings that may feel shameful or too painful to be shared with other people. Through being *held* and *contained* the children learn how to cope with those overwhelming or potentially explosive emotions. This is not something I 'do' to my clients. It is based on a collaborative, witnessing process and it is something you can also learn how to do.

The most effective way to learn how to unpack the children's backpack is to unpack your own first! Completing this experiential exercise will not only give you the framework but also invaluable insight into yourself. You will appreciate the courage it takes to unpack an emotional backpack so that when you ask a child to do this, you will be able to do so with compassion and empathy.

The benefits of unpacking the backpack are:

- The children have more space in their head and heart to hear and listen, to follow instructions, be creative and thoughtful – while the backpack is overflowing, they will struggle to do these things, which can result in a lack of attention in class and general disruptive behaviour. Their work may suffer and their friendships may show signs of strain.
- The teacher is not spending as much time resolving conflict and emotionally caretaking which frees her up to teach.

Learning to unpack and repack your backpack is a five-step process which helps you to identify two things:

- Painful losses which may be affecting your ability to cope
- Resources to help you move forward with making changes

Children carry two backpacks. The visible one which they literally carry on their backs contains their school books and materials, and the invisible one contains their dreams, hopes, fears, worries, anxieties and losses. This exercise involves the children identifying which of those things they no longer want to carry around in their backpack because they are too heavy, and what they need to move forward with. This heaviness will be for one of three reasons:

- X has served its purpose;
- The purpose does not make sense to the children – maybe someone else's expectations;
- The pain of carrying a loss becomes unbearable.

The invisible backpack is similar to a broken heart – we can't literally see it, but we can become aware of the pieces and signs when this backpack gets heavy and burdensome for the children. These signs show up in the form of the children's changed behaviour; their focus and concentration may deteriorate, their sleep pattern may be disrupted, and they may become 'demand resistant'. At this point, it maybe tempting to reach for an ADHD assessment, but I say hold fire on that until you have looked inside their backpack. You maybe surprised by what you find there.

Items you will need for this exercise

The first thing you are going to do is to give the children a small backpack and get them to fill it with stones. You will have collected these stones for your toolkit. Use any type of garden stone, as many as you can fit into your toolkit. If the child needs more stones, have a stack of paper plates available onto which they can write their worries.

Use the questions below to help the children name each stone that they put into the backpack. Some children call the stones, 'homework', 'being told what to do', 'my annoying brother' – you will get a list which will get progressively more serious. This is quite common as the child allows herself to unload her worries and anxieties. Encourage the children to use all the stones and to fill the backpack. Then ask the children to wear the backpack and feel how heavy it is. Next, ask them to remove the backpack and use the questions below as prompts to encourage them to take out the stones that they no longer wants to carry. Have a waste paper bin to hand and let the children drop the stones into the bin. Ask them to tell you how it feels to let go of the stones they no longer need.

This exercise is one which you can return to again and again. You can also complete one step each week for five weeks. It's important to make a start, and to create an awareness with the children about the connection between cause and effect, i.e. by acknowledging the heaviness of their worries they can then begin to understand the impact of those on their behaviour and learn to do something about that, i.e. choosing how they react. That is the sign of resilience and coping that we want to see. That will be the subject of your continuing work together. It would be possible, desirable even, to suggest to the children that you make this exercise part of a weekly game, which would allow them to process their feelings with you and to continue to discover new coping strategies for themselves.

Step 1: What is inside your backpack? Name each stone
What's in your backpack that's affecting your ability to cope with daily life?

- Past experiences – memories, thoughts, images, dwelling on the past.
- Current concerns – life circumstances, worries, anxieties, losses, changes.
- What's fuelling your problems now?
- Future – anxiety about what might happen and your ability to cope.

Step 2: If you could see your backpack, what would it look like? Draw a picture of it

- What colour is it?
- How big is it?
- How do you carry it?
- How is it fastened? How secure does it feel? Does it have a zip, velcro, buttons, straps, padlock, etc?
- How do you know it's your backpack? Does it have your name on it?
- What would cause it to come undone and open up?
- What would others see (about you) when that happens?

Step 3: What does it feel like when you're carrying your backpack? Draw or talk

- What sensations do you feel in your body? Tiredness, headache, heart racing or pounding, breathing changes, shaking, dizzy, light-headed, tense muscles, hot, sweaty, can't concentrate, poor memory, restless, etc.
- What thoughts go through your mind?
- What emotions do you experience?
- What do you do that helps you cope or feel better?

Step 4: What would your ideal backpack look like? How different would this be?

- What would you like to take out of your backpack for good?
- What would your new backpack feel like?
- What colour would you like it to be? How big would it be? How does it fasten? How do you wear it? How heavy would it be? What would be in it? What would you carry?
- What would be most helpful for you to carry with you?

Step 5: Take a different step forward

Now that we know more about your backpack, and how you'd like things to be when you lighten the load of your backpack, make an action plan to start creating the process of change:

- What do I want to stop doing?
- What do I want to do less of?
- What do I want to start doing?
- What do I want to do more of?
- Who can help me to make these changes?

I would not recommend doing this exercise with children who are recently bereaved because it will be too soon for them to access their feelings. You could do this after a few months. If you find that children get stuck at various steps, you could try using a creative visualization exercise with them before moving onto the next step. I find creative visualization very useful with children who may be left-brain dominant because it helps to bypass their rational thinking and takes them directly to their imagination and feelings. This is listed in the appendices.

Ways for teachers to support children through loss and change

- Help the children unpack their backpack – find out how they are feeling: 'How are you feeling about Jane leaving?' 'Will you miss her?' 'What will you miss?' At the same time, try not to probe nor make assumptions about how the child might be feeling.
- For example, reassure the child that their new teacher will make sure they are well cared for and safe. Talk about what will be the same (i.e. friends and other teachers who continue to be with the children.)
- Recommend that parents try to minimize other changes in the child's life for a while: the people, places, routines, and rituals. Try to keep consistent home routines and boundaries.

- Acknowledge and accept the sadness or anger children may feel. 'We all feel sad when someone leaves us. Sometimes you may feel angry that he or she isn't your teacher anymore and that is OK.'
- Ask the child if he or she would like to write a message or draw a picture to send to the teacher who left.
- Find time out to read the child a story.
- Create a boundaried space in the class where the child retreats to go and cool down.

In order to cope with any change, children need to feel supported in that process especially as any change involves some kind of loss, or what I call, 'big little losses' which can get overlooked during the preparations for change.

When losses are not acknowledged a child can feel anxious and stressed which then compounds the issue of transitioning, in any context. Children need boundaries, routine and rituals to help them signpost and feel secure and when these change they need help to create new routines and rituals. Losing the consistency of the routine can be upsetting, especially if the child has become attached to these teachers who leave. At this point their 'backpack' may feel heavier than usual and they will need to unpack this anxiety so that they have more room to cope better by accessing their left side of their brain.

A new teacher is a big change for a child because it means they have to start all over again to build a relationship with that new teacher. I know that many schools do start to prepare children for this transition and the story in this section is designed to be used by teachers to complement their activities especially with children who are particularly sensitive to this change.

Key messages

There are two main messages which adults give to children. Sometimes the denial message can be used if the adult is under time pressure or stress, but the resilient message is the one we need to be aiming to use:

1. A denial message (look how many new and exciting things there are to do here!)
2. A resilient message (I know you really miss your best friend and how difficult this is for you.)

Parents may say the first message if they are feeling guilty and struggling with their feelings, which makes it harder for them to do what I call, the three As:

1. Acknowledge
2. Accept
3. Action

They move quickly to Act before acknowledging the child's feelings and helping them to accept them. If the child doesn't feel her feelings have been fully acknowledged and accepted, this is usually when her behaviour will ramp up. This is code for 'You are not listening to me, pay attention!' The way to de-escalate this behaviour is to acknowledge how the child is feeling first.

I know from parents and teachers in my practice how difficult it is sometimes to stay listening when their child is pushing all their buttons. The main button is the one called, 'I want you to stop hurting'. One of my clients has said that nothing is worse than watching his child struggle and being unable to stop this struggle for them. My point is this, when we try and remove the struggle we also remove the children's right to have their feelings and to find their own solutions. If we impose a solution on the children, we risk them missing out on this valuable learning – how to discover their own solutions. Sometimes adults impose solutions with the best intentions but usually there is an element of being unable to tolerate their own discomfort. In my view, this discomfort is not their children's problem. The adult has to learn how to tolerate their discomfort and to help support their children in their struggle for answers.

What we need to do is to acknowledge they are struggling and accept the pain this is causing them, and we do this by doing what Carl Rogers called 'active listening'. So in the midst of a struggle, we can start by asking children questions., such as: *What do you need from me right now, in this situation?*' And then wait for the answer! Carl Rogers and Richard Farson coined the term 'active listening' in 1957 in a paper of the same title (reprinted in 1987 in the volume *Communicating in Business Today*). 'Active listening' is an important way to bring about changes in people. Despite the popular notion that listening is a passive approach, clinical and research evidence clearly shows that sensitive listening is a most effective agent for individual personality change and group development.

Active listening requires that the listener fully concentrate, understand, respond and then remember what is being said. This is opposed to reflective listening where the listeners repeats back to the speaker what they have just heard to confirm understanding of both parties.

I use active listening in my work with families, especially parents who are at the end of their patience with their child's ramped up behaviour. I usually start by asking them: '*What do you think your child is trying to tell you based on what you hear?*'

Nine times out of ten the parents are shocked when we have drilled down on this question to find what the child is really trying to say! Once they have 'got it', parents are more equipped to cope with the ups and downs of their child's emotions.

Active listening is particularly challenging for busy, stressed parents and teachers because so often they are operating in 'fix-it' mode which is all about taking action. We need to find a way to slow things down during communication so that we can actively listen and hear what the children are saying or communicating through their behaviour.

Patty Wipfler and Tosha Schore, authors of the book *Listen*, call this practice 'stay listening' which means listening all the way through your child's upset. If your child is crying, stay with them instead of giving them a fix-it solution: if you stop crying we can go and get ice-cream, for example. I know that it can be tough to slow down communication in a busy classroom which is why I hope using the story 'The egg without a shell' will be a useful tool for when there is time outside the classroom to spend one-to-one with the child. And in most cases, the most useful tool will be the three As: Acknowledge, Accept, Act.

* * * * * * * * * * * * * * * * * * * *

Aggression after a teacher leaves school

Billy was one of my most challenging cases. He was 8 years old when he was referred to me by a head teacher because of his angry meltdowns. I knew from reading the referral that Billy was in a lot of pain and was trying to bring attention to this. No one seemed to understand why. Looking back, the clues were there all along.

On the surface Billy was angry about leaving his teacher to move into the next school year and had become very disruptive in his class: standing up during his lessons, shouting at other pupils, and kicking waste paper baskets. After 12 play therapy sessions, it was clear that Billy was also angry with other people in his young life: his parents (who were divorced and fought a lot and had made him move house) and his younger sister who constantly annoyed him by 'stealing my toys and messing up my stuff'. At school Billy was always getting into trouble: Billy was at the centre of any playground disruption, the first to complain and needing to have the last word. Any timetable change would send Billy into a meltdown and it could take several hours for him to self-regulate. Billy was being triggered by these changes. I worked hard to hold and contain Billy's anger so that he could feel safe enough to express this without fear, and over time, he learnt how to express his real needs: consistency and routine. It was important to Billy to find the toys in the same place each week, to have his weekly session at the same time and to hear me count down from 10 to 0 so he knew his session had ended. Small things were big things for Billy: walking into his session and noticing his special box was sitting in the same place at the end of the table reassured him and helped build trust between us.

After every session with Billy I felt physically hungry and tired, evidence of how deep Billy's needs also were. Billy taught me how to be a better therapist because together we figured out that underneath Billy's anger were his feelings of sadness about his losses: his family unit, his family home, everything familiar to him which made him feel secure.

Theory

According to Bright Horizons, Family Solutions there are four pillars of security in a child's life:

1. People: attachment figures – those whom children rely on for strength and reassurance.
2. Place: the familiar settings where children feel comfortable and safe.
3. Routine: the regular, dependable daily plan such as how a teacher conducts circle time or prepares a snack.
4. Ritual: comforting traditions like singing a 'Good Morning' song everyday as children sit in their favourite spot. I have known children in this context to get very upset if another child is in their special place, an indication of the sensitivity some children can feel towards change. If children can resolve this issue themselves it's usually a sign that they have enough resilience and inner resources to cope with this type of change but if they get upset, it can be a sign that they are struggling with separation anxiety of some form.

All four of these pillars had been threatened in Billy's life, and his teacher's departure was the final straw.

Losing a teacher occurs in three different phases of a child's school life:

- A teacher leaves the school.
- Transitioning from pre-school to primary school. In the US, a child loses a teacher every school year.
- Transitioning from primary to secondary school.

In this book I am focusing on the first phase. Much has been written about 'School readiness' for transitioning from pre-school to primary and from primary to secondary school.

Teachers leave for two primary reasons: a job change or personal circumstances. If those personal circumstances include an illness which results in death, then the impact of that loss on the child might be significantly deeper than if the teacher simply leaves the school to take up a position in another school. In the latter situation the children will understand that although they will no longer see their teacher every day, the teacher still exists, whereas if the teacher dies, the children's loss and the impact of that loss may take several years to process.

Very often in primary school, a child will become attached to a teacher and find the separation from that teacher problematic. The reaction of a child differs depending upon his/her age, temperament, environment, and parents' reactions. Some children feel loss more deeply and take longer to adjust to change. When a teacher leaves, the new reality is not just the absence of the former teacher but also the presence of someone new.

The prospect of having to navigate the daily decisions without the support of a familiar figure can be traumatic for some children. In this age group the children may be starting to articulate this anxiety directly to their parents, but for some children, acting this anxiety out in the form of aggression is the way they get attention brought to them.

Story 2.1 When Sam's teacher left school

Sam was 8 years old when his favourite teacher moved away. Suddenly, Sam's small world got even smaller as he felt lost and lonely.

Before the teacher left, Sam had enjoyed the morning ritual of singing the class song, 'Hello New Day'. The class had created the song by first drawing pictures about what a new day felt like and Jack had then encouraged them to put words to these pictures. Their music teacher, Mrs Phelps, had come in specially to help them make a tune out of their words. Sam's goal each day was to get to school early enough so that he could sit in the same place ready to sing their song each day knowing that he would feel good afterwards about getting on with his work. Now he felt sad about having to get used to a new teacher. Would they still be able to sing their song? Sam wondered. His heart felt heavy.

The other ritual the class had was called 'unpacking my backpack' which they did at the end of the day before going home. His teacher explained that just as children carried a physical backpack full of books, they also carried an invisible one, full of their worries. The children sat in a circle on the floor and the teacher asked them what worries they wanted to take out of their backpacks. When Sam unpacked his backpack he felt much lighter and skipped to the school gate to meet his Mum.

Sam liked the fact that his teacher never got angry with him, even when he and his friends were noisy. Instead he would give them a one-minute warning and then they had to settle down, but Sam's backpack was starting to feel heavy when he thought about his teacher leaving and he started pushing against the one-minute warning.

Sam suddenly felt really cross and angry. 'You don't care about us,' Sam yelled at his teacher, 'you're leaving!' he shouted and threw his exercise books onto the floor.

Sam's teacher asked him to pick up his books and said, 'Can we talk about this Sam at the end of the day please?'

The next day at school Sam got into a fight with another boy in the playground over not sharing his sweets. Sam felt like hoarding his sweets and stuffed them in his pocket to hide them. He hoped no one had noticed. He was saving them to give to his teacher at the end of the day as a parting gift, something to remember him by. Sam felt scared his teacher would forget all about him.

'Sam, you have got more sweets than me, give me some of yours so it's fair,' said Tom.

'No I haven't,' said Sam defensively as he jammed his hand into his pockets to feel the sweets.

'Oh yes you have!' Tom shouted. Other children stopped what they were doing and wandered over to where Sam and Tom were now standing very close to each other. Sam pushed the sweets into his pocket corners.

'So what if I have?' Sam taunted. 'They are MY sweets, not yours, and I don't want to share them with you,' he flared.

Tom's face twisted in anger. 'Who are you saving them for then, your girlfriend?' and laughed in Sam's face. Sam felt his face flush, he felt embarrassed to say he was saving them for his teacher, so instead he pushed Tom in the chest. Tom wobbled backwards but recovered quickly before pushing Sam back, really hard so that he fell over backwards.

The break time supervisor heard the noise level rising as the other children started to goad on the boys to 'fight, fight, fight'.

'OK everyone,' she said calmly. 'The fight is over. Please step back now and carry on with your play. I want to speak to Sam and Tom now in my office.'

Both boys were red in the face but followed the supervisor to her office.

The teacher was told about the incident and before the end of the day he asked Sam to sit with him in his office which was quiet. 'Sam, you know the drill,' said the teacher. 'We don't physically hurt each other, ever. You can hit the floor, but you can't physically push anyone else. Why don't you tell me what happened?' he said. Sam recounted the story, while staring at the floor. He felt deeply ashamed to have let his teacher down.

'I'm wondering about your backpack,' said the teacher. 'How is that feeling at the moment?' he said.

Sam looked up at his teacher and uncrossed his arms. He sank a bit further into the chair.

'Dunno,' he said, fiddling with some string he had taken out of his pocket. He swung his legs back and forth under the chair.

'You sounded pretty upset in the playground,' his teacher said.

'Yeah, I was,' said Sam still swinging his legs. He looked at his teacher's red socks. Sam suddenly felt overwhelmingly sad about not seeing his red socks every day.

'Your socks,' said Sam quietly. 'I will miss your socks.'

His teacher looked down at his red socks.

'I don't want you to leave,' said Sam, his voice sounding flat.

'Is that what is making you angry?' said his teacher.

Sam was embarrassed but his teacher wasn't cross with him and he said it in a quiet voice which always encouraged Sam.

'I didn't mean to hurt Tom,' said Sam.

'I understand how that happens when we are feeling strong emotions,' said the teacher. 'Me leaving the school is a big change in your life and it makes me feel sad too,' he said.

Sam looked a bit brighter. He didn't feel so alone now if his teacher felt the same as he did.

'I've got an idea,' said the teacher. 'I know how much you enjoy signing our Hello New Day song. Would you like to create a Farewell song for me, and ask the rest of your class to help with this? You could go into the music pod to do this, if you like,' said the teacher.

Sam lifted his head up and stopped swinging his legs.

'Could we use the drums?' he said.

'Of course!' said his teacher, 'they would sound amazing. Before you go back to your class, have a think about who else might like to help you create this.'

This stopped Sam in his tracks. Rats. He was just getting excited about this idea, and a bit scared that no one would want to help him after the playground fight.

The next day at school Sam asked his friend Jess if he wanted to help with the Farewell song.

'Sure,' he said. 'I can play the keyboard and we can practice at my house, if you like,' Jess said. Tom was standing close by and overhead the conversation.

'Can I play in the song?' said Tom. 'Always wanted to play in a band.'

'We aren't making a band,' said Sam quickly, 'we are making a Farewell song for our teacher,' he said. 'What can you do, sing or play?' he said, hoping that Tom would say neither.

'Drums,' said Tom, 'my big brother had a set for his birthday and he lets me play them sometimes, they make a loud noise!' he said grinning.

'Oh wow, said Jess, 'drums would be great!' 'And what about Jack, I know he plays the trumpet' said Jess. Sam started to feel excited! They had a keyboard, drums and a trumpet. The sound would knock his teacher's red socks right off! The playground fight was forgotten.

'OK,' said Sam, 'let's meet at my house after tea tonight, shall we?'

All three boys grinned at each other.

What can I do to help?

Questions to ask

- What will you miss most about your teacher? (offer paper and crayons)
- What song reminds you of your teacher? (offer to listen to this with them)

Key messages

Be aware of the denial message that you may want to use to try and comfort the child. This won't help because this does not acknowledge their loss. Instead, use the resilient message, which acknowledges their loss and tells them that they will survive this.

The denial message: I'm sure you will like your new teacher.
The resilient message: Your teacher will always hold a special place in your heart. How would you like to remember him/her?

Classroom activity

Appetizer: Musical chairs

This exercise requires two chairs and some musical instruments. I recommend a small drum and stick, a rattle, triangle and a thunder tube which is a percussion instrument and the most popular instrument in my play therapy kit.

Collect the instruments together and place these on a small table near the child. Invite him to select one instrument from the table and choose a chair to sit on. You then do the same.

Put a timer on the desk and set it for 5 minutes. At this point you and the child should be sitting opposite one another holding your musical instrument. When you activate the timer, you have 5 minutes in which to use the chosen instrument. Tell the child that he or she is in charge when you change chairs. At the point of changing chairs, he can also choose another musical instrument to use. Repeat this until the 5 minute timer goes off.

The point of this exercise is to let the child let off steam in a contained fashion. The sound of music can literally match the children's emotions so this may be loud or soft depending on how they are feeling. They will get into this exercise quickly and, more so if you show them how 'up for it' you are. You can do this through your facial expression and body language.

Once the 5 minutes is up, ask the children to return to the table where the musical instruments are and invite them to name each instrument in their own words. What does this instrument evoke for them? By doing this they are starting to learn how to name their feelings.

Main course: 4-part pizza or Unpacking the backpack

* *

Anger after the death of a friend

CASE STUDY 2.2

Evan was 6 years old when he was referred to me by his primary school teacher. She was concerned about some of his behaviours which seemed uncharacteristic. He had started pinching other children. The children he was pinching were upset and told Evan to stop but this seemed to anger Evan until he eventually burst into tears literally in a heap on the floor. After I consulted Evan's parents they told me that Evan had recently lost his best friend Joe, who had died suddenly in a car accident. The whole school was affected by Joe's death but for Evan this loss was particularly tough as his grandad had died the year before. The family were grieving heavily and found it difficult to cope with Evan's behaviour which they were calling 'challenging'. This amounted to Evan pushing all their patience buttons and having angry meltdowns when his needs were not immediately met. The parents were at their wits end.

Working with grieving children is like peeling back the layers on an onion. The first layer was Evan talking about Joe, but then he quickly moved onto the more routine issues that bothered him at school, before circling back to Joe. His loss was held in little pockets inside him and together we slowly unpacked these over many weeks through creating paintings and clay models, until Evan was ready to leave the safety of his play therapy room. I always know when children are ready to leave because they start to self-direct their play which is what Evan started to do. This is a healthy sign that the child has taken enough in through the play and stored those resources inside them, ready to use in the outside world.

I always give a child in play therapy a small empty shoe box in which they can keep the objects they make in their sessions. The objects are symbolic of the resources they are finding within themselves. Evan filled several boxes with his drawings, paintings and clay models, and letters to Joe. On his final day, we carefully packed his boxes into a large plastic holdall which he took home, and according to his parents, he kept this in his bedroom and took it out sometimes before bedtime to look at.

Sometimes Evan and I talked about his drawings but often we didn't. The act of creating the drawing was enough for him, and he would carefully place these inside his box. Children in play therapy intuitively know what they need and are very skilled at showing you through the creative mediums, which is why I believe the stories are useful tools to use with children who are stuck in their grief.

Theory

According to Cruse Bereavement, anger is a common response to bereavement amongst children. Compounding this is the fact that bereaved children can find it difficult to understand their emotions and verbally articulate how they are feeling, so their anger can sometimes be expressed indirectly through acting out.

They can also feel angry with people they feel did not do enough to prevent their loved one from dying. A child might be extremely angry towards the nurses who cared for his mother whilst she was dying believing that their care was inadequate or lacking in some way and that was why his mother died.

Quite common is the anger a child or young person feels towards the person who has died. This anger can be directed at the person who has died for not allowing the child or young person the time to say goodbye, or it could be because the child or young person feels that they have been abandoned by the person dying. Anger can also be directed at the person who has died because their death has left the child or young person to deal with the strong emotions that grief entails by themselves.

Anger can manifest itself in various ways according to the child or young person's understanding of death at the time of the bereavement. Younger children may have tantrums and become aggressive towards others; older children might become disruptive at school and get in to fights with other children.

Anger is an understandable response to bereavement and it is something that the majority of children and young people will experience as they grieve.

Story 2.2 Seeing red

Billy was always getting into trouble at school. He spent a lot of time in class detention.

Billy felt lonely. Since his best friend Monty died he had no one to talk to about stuff. Monty and Billy shared a love of trees. During break time, when other children were racing around the playground, Billy and Monty were having a competition about how many different shades of green they could see.

His Mum and Dad told him that he would eventually get over his sadness but Billy wondered how he was meant to do that, and what did 'getting over it' mean anyway? He felt frustrated that no one could explain that to him. Did they mean that he would be over Monty when he stopped thinking about him?

Didn't they understand that Monty was his best friend! They went on family holidays together every year – no one understood Billy's fascination with snails as much as Monty did. Their snail hunting trips were their weekend ritual and their collection was the only thing Billy now had left of Monty. As he looked at the collection Billy wished he had told Monty how much those trips meant to him.

In his bedroom at night he'd say out loud:

'Why didn't I die with you in that car crash Monty?! Why you and not me?'

At school Billy's teacher noticed how angry he got if something didn't go his way or, if Billy lost at a game in class. Billy's face would turn bright red as he struggled to control himself before he burst out:

'It's not fair, why am I always the one who loses?' before sweeping his pen and pencils off his desk onto the floor.

No one in the class knew what to say to Billy when he was angry to make things better for him. Immediately afterwards Billy would go quiet as he felt the shame of his angry outburst. Inside Billy's tummy was rumbling and upset.

His teacher tried to calm Billy down, but Billy pushed his chair away from his desk and stood up, fighting back his tears. He didn't want them to drop in front of his friends; he was scared they would laugh at him. He looked at his teacher.

'I tell you what, Billy, why don't you go outside and sit on the chair in the hallway?' she said.

Billy wandered outside and stood with his back to the wall, one foot against it, hands in his pockets. The autumn wind was chilly. His boots felt heavy.

The big oak tree standing in the middle of the school's garden suddenly looked very big to Billy. It was covered with thousands of green leaves – he started to count the different shades of green until he noticed something different – were some of them red, he wondered.

One of the leaves looked like a bright red apple! His Mum sometimes made him baked apples for when Monty came round for his tea, and added ice-cream when he got a good report, which wasn't very often these days. Since Monty died Billy couldn't concentrate as well on his school work. Apples reminded Billy of Monty. Billy suddenly felt hungry for his Mum's baked apples.

Maybe if he had a closer look at the tree he'd be able to pick some apples to give to his Mum, and he could ask her to bake them for tea!

Billy felt excited again.

He took a quick look into the classroom and saw his teacher writing on the backboard. She'd never notice he'd gone …

Billy sprinted across the quad, and slowed down as he approached the garden of oak trees. Monty's favourite tree, he thought wistfully. All the leaves had turned red! Bright as a neon sign. Billy wondered if he was in the wrong place, but before he could run away, he heard a voice say:

'Hello Billy, I've been waiting to meet you,' she said.

Billy jumped about five feet into the air.

'Who's that?' he asked.

'It's me. Dilly Dangle.'

Billy turned around so he could see where the voice was coming from.

Dilly had removed her hat and revealed her long flame red hair which unfurled almost to the ground.

'Here I am, Billy.'

Billy looked dazed and was lost for words.

'It's OK, Billy, I'm not here to tell you off. I'm here to tell you that I know how sad you are about losing Monty,' she said.

'I'm not sad,' said Billy, 'I'm angry – why has he left me alone?' Billy cried.

'Sit down and get comfortable Billy,' said Dilly.

Billy plonked himself on the ground which had suddenly become dry instead of muddy, and felt soft like a velvet carpet. Billy felt comfortable sitting there.

'When you get these feelings, do you notice anything else right before you get them?' asked Dilly.

Billy closed his eyes as he thought for a second.

'Yes!' he said. 'I get a jangly feeling in my tummy, and sometimes my head hurts, or my nose itches,' he said. 'I just see red! And before I know it I am feeling very cross.

'That's me Billy trying to get your attention. When you feel jangly that's because I am trying to tell you something,' explained Dilly.

Billy looked intrigued.

'You mean you are the one who warns me because sometimes I see a little red light flashing, and I can't stop it,' he said.

'Yes, Billy, that's me, I'm dangling from this tree to get your attention because I want you to stop and listen,' Dilly said.

Billy looked like a light had been switched on inside him. He stood up and walked closer to Dilly.

'I'm your friend, Billy. You can come and talk to me anytime,' said Dilly.

Billy put his head on one side, listening intently.

'Anger is like an iceberg, Billy. These jangly, red feelings are just the tip that you and everyone else sees, but underneath the ice there are others, and these are called frustration and helplessness,' she said.

The wind rustled the leaves. Suddenly Billy could feel Monty's presence. He couldn't see him but he felt he was nearby. He didn't feel scared, just intrigued.

'You feel frustrated that Monty has left you – he died and you didn't, and that makes you feel helpless. The world now feels like a scary place. Does that make sense?' Dilly said.

'Yes, it does,' said Billy. 'But I don't know how to tell people about those other feelings below the ice,' he said. 'They just see me being angry and run away from me, and I don't want them to,' he said.

'I understand that, Billy, and to help you get started I'm giving you three blank cards. When you are feeling overwhelmed and seeing red, I want you to hold up one of the cards and show your teacher,' she said. 'This is your tool for letting her know what you are feeling below your iceberg. She will then be able to suggest that you take some time out and go to your play box,' she said. 'Playing there for half an hour will help you to calm your iceberg down,' she said.

Billy suddenly felt better than he had done in ages. Someone had heard him! He liked the sound of the play box and took the cards from Dilly and put them in his pocket.

'Keep those cards safe, Billy, they are your ticket to melting your iceberg,' she said.

Billy nodded. 'Thank you, Dilly' he said. He got up to go back to class and as he turned around to say goodbye to Dilly he noticed that all the leaves had turned green and were gently swaying in the breeze.

Billy touched the cards in his pocket and felt happy knowing they were safe and that he had more colours and words for expressing his feelings. Maybe he would add a fourth card and colour this green, and always keep this in his pocket to remind him of Dilly. Billy looked up at the tree and thought he could see the leaves smiling at him.

What can I do to help?

One way we can support children who are angry and acting out is to explain to them that anger has its origin in several other emotions that are felt long before anger is expressed. Anger is so powerful that it often overwhelms these 'first emotions' (D. Sims Darcie, *Anger and Grief in Children*). There is a hierarchy to anger:

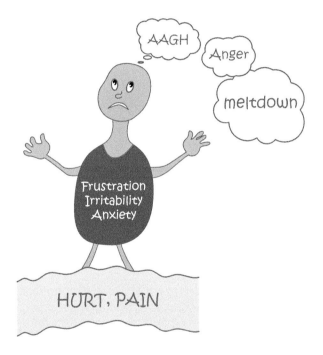

Underneath anger is frustration and at the bottom is hurt. If this hurt goes unacknowledged, that produces frustration, which can quickly turn into anger. I see children whose angry behaviour escalates at school for no apparent rational reason. Usually the escalation is produced by the children feeling their concerns are not being acknowledged. I explain to parents and teachers that it is common for children who feel this frustration to ratchet up their behaviour as a way of getting someone's attention. The children's inner narrative will go something like this: 'If only you understood how frustrated I felt.' Often, underneath the frustration is a sense of helplessness. A sudden death can produce a sense of helplessness. No one likes to feel helpless, so that feeling can be quickly converted into anger. Helplessness is a weak feeling; one without controls or power. Sometimes children feeling helpless can become overly controlling in other areas of their life, as a way of dialling back their sense of helplessness.

- If a child or young person's anger is causing them to hurt themselves or others explain to them that it is OK to feel angry but not OK to hurt themselves or other people. This may be the point at which to seek external intervention and assessment.
- Encourage the child or young person to vent their anger towards a pillow or to go for a run; any physical activity that will enable them to push the stress out of their body should be helpful. Anything that will allow the child or young person to channel their anger in a safe way can be used.
- Reassure the child or young person that it is OK to feel anger towards the person who has died and that this is a natural response and not something they should feel guilty about.
- If the child or young person's anger is directed towards you, try not to take it personally. Often children and young people will direct their anger at the person they feel closest to. By remaining constant and not getting upset by the child or young person's anger you are reinforcing the fact that you will be there for them no matter what.
- **Model appropriate ways to express frustration.** For example, if you are having trouble with putting something together, or, if you spill something, take time to explain what you are finding frustrating.
- **Anticipate difficulties.** Notice when children are losing interest or tiring of an activity, and ask them what else they would prefer to do instead.

Questions to ask

- What colours would you choose if you were feeling angry?
- In which part of your body do you feel angry?

Key messages

- **The denial message:** You have lots of other friends to play with (this closes the issue down).
- **The resilient message:** The death of a friend is equivalent to the loss of a limb – German proverb. What would help you to remember your friend? (this opens up the chance for expression and healing).

Classroom activity

Appetizer: Pound out your frustration!

A small play dough or clay table is a great place for a child to go and 'pound out' her frustrations. Add to this a small box, shoe box size, to contain whatever object the child makes in the play dough or clay. Inside the box place a pack of six coloured blank cards. After the child has finished making a clay object, invite them to write down any words to describe their feelings towards the clay object. The child can either take the object home with them, or keep it inside the box which you could then store safely in the classroom. The advantage of doing this is that if you do need to repeat this exercise, the child can add objects to the box. Be sure to explain that once the box is full, the exercise will stop. This creates a useful boundary for the child.

Main course: Four-part pizza

* * * * * * * * * * * * * * * * * * * *

Anxiety after the death of a pet

Ellie was 8 years of age when Norris, her beloved cat, died, and she was referred to me for play therapy by her Mum. Ellie was struggling with her loss and grief which showed up in her increased anxiety, at home and at her primary school.

Ellie became anxious if she had to leave her classroom alone to go to the toilet. At home she had difficult going upstairs alone at any time, day and night. This had become a problem for her Mum who also had a young baby to take care of. Ellie's Dad had a full-time job outside the home so the responsibility for child care was mainly down to Ellie's Mum. Ellie had become clingy when faced with separation from her Mum; during school morning drop off particularly, she would cry and cling to her Mum's legs.

In her early play therapy sessions Ellie did not talk directly about Norris. It was around session 4, when mutual trust and rapport had been established between us, that she buried a cat in the sand and placed a small child figure beside the cat's grave. The silence in the room was palpable. Ellie sat very quietly for several minutes stroking the sand on top of the cat and around his grave. It was then that she told me that Norris had died. He had been hit by a car and a stranger had found him by the roadside.

'That must have been quite a shock,' I said out loud.

Ellie nodded, keeping her eyes and hands in the sand.

We sat closely together on the floor. I let the space hold Ellie's thoughts until she was ready to show me what she wanted to do next. She stopped stroking the sand and let her fingers trail lightly through the sand until they reached the edge of the sand tray.

'I wonder where Norris is now and when I lie in bed at night I am scared to close my eyes,' she said.

'You are scared to close your eyes,' I mirrored back to her.

'Yes, I am,' she said.

'What do you imagine will happen if you close your eyes?' I said.

'I'm scared I might die too,' she said and looked directly at me for the first time.

'I can hear that your fear feels real, Ellie,' I said.

Once Ellie had voiced her real fear out loud she was able to accept this and move on. Afterwards her body movement was different, less jerky; she moved around the room more easily instead of darting from one creative medium to the next. A child's movement is often a reflection of their feelings and I took this change in Ellie's movement as a sign of the internal shift that had taken place after the voicing of her fears (Jean Newlove and John Dalby, 2007, *Laban for All*, London: Nick Hern Books). Rudolf Laban is one of the great theorists and practitioners of movement. He laid down a system for analysing the way the human being moves in space, based on three parts: the body, direction and quality of movement. He ascribed values to these movements, releasing the expressive power contained within each of them. When I am observing movement in my clients, I defer to Laban, who argues that movement inspires accompanying moods which are felt more or less strongly according to the degree of effort applied (Newlove and Dalby, 2007, p. 102).

For example, Laban described jerky movements as 'broken flow' (Sherborne, p. 58). When children are feeling frustrated and restless, their movements can become sudden, and they may resort to flicking toys or sometimes other children. An abrupt change from one effort, for example slow gliding, to its complete contrast, rapid jerky movements, indicates discord in the mental and bodily state of the child (Newlove and Dalby, 2007, p. 102). When we acknowledge these abrupt movement changes to children, in a non-judgemental way, we are able to help them make use of a harmonious transition from one effort to the other. For example, 'Tommy, I am noticing that you have started to move around more quickly and I'm wondering about what prompted that change?' The key to making this acknowledgement is to ask an open ended question rather than a closed one because we are inviting the child to open up to us. If we ask them a closed question, we are likely to get a shrug of their shoulder or, 'I don't know' in response. This doesn't mean the child has no opinion on the matter, only that we haven't created a space for them to come into. The more playful you make this question, the more likely the child is going to engage with you.

Most childhood fears represent a deeper unexpressed fear. If we don't give grieving children the space to voice their fears one way of them dealing with this is to subvert them into monsters (Dennis McCarthy, 2007, 'If you turned into a monster': Transformation through Play: A Body-centred Approach to Play Therapy, London: Jessica Kingsley), which can appear in their nightmares and feel real. Other ways they subvert fears is to avoid and shut down talking about subjects, so they may appear sullen and uncommunicative. A fear of spiders is very common in my practice. I now treat these fears as the child's way of flagging up their unexpressed fears and invite them to tell me more about the spider – 'Where does he live? 'Does he have any friends?' etc. The object itself isn't really important, this is just the vehicle the child has chosen to project their fear onto, so don't waste time rescuing them from the spider! Instead, have fun with this, be playful in your enquiry, start a dialogue about the spider – enter your child's imagination and let them reveal what's really frightening them.

I agree with McCarthy when he says that children come into therapy with monstrous feelings – monstrous grief, rage, longing, to name a few. When they draw monsters or place them into the sand tray, I know that they are feeling some of those monstrous feelings. Once those monsters have been excavated, i.e. represented and expressed, part of the child's self, which has been repressed or never developed, can start to emerge. Interestingly, the fear of spiders then tends to recede! This is a transformative process for children – the child no longer needs to project the fear onto an external object – the internal work has been done and they can move on. Similarly, children bring these monsters into school, and they can trigger an emotional response during conflict or confrontation. Seeing a child in the classroom who might be struggling with his/her inner demons and monsters is a signpost to offer a creative intervention such as a therapeutic story using the adapted 6PSM.

Following Ellie's acknowledgement of her fear we were able to more forward together and explore her taking risks, which proved that she could step outside and beyond her fear. Initially these were tentative steps – choosing different coloured paints, arranging objects in different orders, playing musical instruments loudly instead of softly, until she ventured into creating her own games for us both to play, assigning us roles and using the entire floor space of the room rather than just a corner, where she originally felt safe. Ellie was expanding herself literally into a bigger space and the more she did this, and trusted me to expand alongside her, the more Ellie's anxiety decreased at home and at school.

Chapter 2

Theory

The death of a pet is a very challenging event in young children's lives and they need guidance from their teachers, parents or grandparents to help them make sense of this loss.

The loss of a pet is often a child's first experience with death, and the circumstances of the death, whether it was from old age or a sudden accident, will affect the way a child grieves the loss. If a pet is terminally ill, parents can help prepare the child by talking about the impending loss, as well as the feelings of sadness this loss will evoke for them.

According to Abigail Marks, a clinical psychologist in San Francisco who specializes in childhood grief, when pets died in tragic and unexpected ways, the loss was harder for the child to accept. This is because the suddenness highlights the unpredictability of the world for the child and can make them feel insecure; suddenly nothing feels certain nor safe.

For only children, losing a pet can be especially devastating. I have seen this in my practice, where the child builds a strong attachment to the pet. This is borne out by Joshua Russell, an assistant professor of environmental science at Canisius College in Buffalo, who has studied the effects of pet loss in children. He explained that for many children, pets become more than just animals. 'Many kids describe their pets as siblings or best friends with whom they have strong connections,' he said.

In a study of 12 children ages 6 to 13 who had lost a pet, published in the journal *Environmental Education Research*, Dr Russell found that even years after the pet's death, some children still described the loss as 'the worst day of their lives'. I have also heard parents refer to the pain of losing pets in their childhood, the memory of which has stayed with them into adulthood.

A child's age and developmental level affect how he or she understands death, and a child's grief looks very different from an adult's. Children do not always cry or immediately show emotion. But this does not mean they are not deeply affected by the loss. Parents often say to me, 'he seems fine, he hasn't cried at all'. I gently explain that this can signify that the child is holding in their sadness or, may not feel able to show their feelings, in some cases for fear of upsetting their parents.

'Kids under the age of 5 will have a hard time understanding that the pet is gone forever because it's difficult for them to grasp the concept of death', said Jessica Harvey, a psychotherapist in San Francisco who specializes in pet grief.

School-age children will often have questions about the animal's death, and the back and forth that ensues may open up larger conversations about love, loss and what happens after we die. When telling a school-age child about a pet's death, Dr Marks recommends being honest about what happened. Doing so lets a child know that it is not taboo to talk about death or painful feelings, which can set the stage to process other sorts of loss in the future. Parents should also validate any emotions that arise as the child mourns.

Dr Marks said it was also important for parents to follow their child's lead. 'If they are asking about the details of the pet's death, it's a sign that they want to talk about it', she said. 'They are looking for your comfort.'

For many children, it is also important to have a goodbye ritual. 'Rituals around death are some of the most meaningful ways we have of recognizing someone's life, but these ceremonies aren't societally defined for pet death', Dr Marks said. Families can create their own rituals, like having a small memorial service, scattering the pet's ashes, planting a remembrance tree or creating a photo album.

'This is a way to process the loss and to honor the role that the pet had in your family,' Dr Marks said.

Increased anxiety

This can manifest in different ways in children: loss of appetite, loss of sleep, lack of interest in playing games or attending school, lack of interest in being sociable, and these are some of the signs to look out for in children, because this is their way of flagging up their anxiety. However, it's not the issue per se that we need to focus on; doing so may only make this worse. For example, getting tough with the child about finishing their food may only exacerbate the issue for them. What they want is for us to help them acknowledge their feelings which are driving their behaviour, so the sadness and loneliness they may feel as a result of losing their pet is acknowledged and processed.

Story 2.3 Come into the garden Maud

Maud hadn't picked up her dog's lead for weeks. It lay on the table by the door under some magazines. Her little Jack Russell had been hit by a car and had died instantly while she was at school. When he did not rush out to meet her from school that day, Maud ran into the kitchen, 'Where's Jack?' she said to her Mum. Her Mum looked sad, and Maud's sixth sense kicked in and told her that something bad had happened to Jack. Her Mum never looked like that at her.

Maud's Mum took a deep breath. 'I'm so sorry, Maud, but Jack has been hit by a car and he's dead. He died instantly, so I don't think he suffered,' she said. She knelt down and held Maud's small hands. 'I know how much you loved Jack, how important he was to you sweetheart.' Maud felt her heart was going to break into pieces.

Jack was a gift from her parents on her eighth birthday. When Maud opened the bow on his blue basket and looked into his brown eyes, she fell instantly in love. He was cute and intelligent and they had a special rapport.

As a puppy Jack didn't sleep very well at nights, so Maud eventually lifted him up onto her bed, and ever after he snuggled down beside her and went to sleep. As an only child, Jack became a special part of Maud's small world. She didn't know if she would ever have a brother or a sister, so Jack became her companion. He had his own basket in her room, and little square blankets in Maud's places in the house so that he could be near her.

When Maud did her piano practice, Jack lay beside her on his blanket, his ears wiggling when she hit a high note! And when Maud sat at her table eating her boiled eggs and toast, Jack beside her ready for the piece of toast Maud would sneak him under the table, so her Mum didn't see! When it rained and thundered at night, Maud was never afraid because Jack lay next to her, his warm little body felt like a hot water bottle.

Maud told Jack how she dreamed of having a hammock in the garden for them both to sleep in so they could look at the stars in the night sky, and how one day they would travel the world together.

The following day, Maud didn't want to go to school, and so her Mum explained to Maud's teacher why Maud was sad. Maud sat in her classroom, at her desk, but her mind kept wandering to Jack – where was he, what he was doing, and could he see how sad she felt. *Was he missing her too?* she wondered.

Maud said that she wanted to bury Jack in the garden, next to the mulberry tree her Mum had planted on Jack's first birthday. So together they prepared the ground, and her Dad carefully carried Jack and laid him in the ground. Maud stood beside her Dad and placed Jack's collar beside his body. As her Dad covered Jack with earth, her Mum held Maud's hand, and the sun came out.

Over the next few weeks Maud's teacher noticed that Maud was anxious about going out to play, and she jumped at hearing the sound of the lunch time bell. Her friends tried to cheer Maud up, but her teacher found Maud alone in the classroom during her break, tidying up the dressing up box, getting upset because all the clothes were in the wrong order. When all the clothes had been folded and tidied Maud's teacher asked Maud if she was ready to go outside and play with her friends. Maud shook her head and her eyes filled with tears. Her teacher sat down next to Maud and held her hand.

'Your Mum told me about Jack dying. I'm so sorry, Maud, I know how much Jack meant to you.'

Maud felt relieved that someone was talking to her directly about Jack. 'He was my best friend,' said Maud, 'I feel so lost without him.'

'I understand,' said her teacher. 'I lost my dog when I was your age so I know how painful this loss is. I felt sad for a very long time and I imagined that he would keep coming into the room,' she said.

'That happens to me too,' said Maud. 'Jack always used to run out to meet me from school, wagging his tail and now he's not there.' She broke off and started to cry again.

Her teacher gently put her arm around Maud and said, 'It's ok to be sad, Maud. I believe that our sadness is our way of showing how much we loved our pets,' she said.

'Really?' said Maud, looking up and wiping her eyes.

'Yes,' said her teacher.

Can I tell you what helped me?' she said.

Maud nodded.

'Drawing pictures of my dog really helped me to remember him,' said her teacher.

Maud looked up. 'I'm so scared of forgetting what Jack looks like,' she said through her sobs. Her teacher leaned in and Maud accepted the comfort.

After a few quiet minutes, her teacher said, 'Would you like me to get you some paper and crayons for you to start drawing some pictures of Jack?' she said.

Maud nodded again.

Over the next few days Maud stayed in at break time and drew pictures of Jack. The dressing up box remained messy but Maud wasn't bothered anymore. The magic of seeing Jack alive again on her pages was a huge comfort.

That night, Maud dreamt that she heard Jack calling out to her: 'Come into the garden, Maud', he said. When Maud woke up she got straight out of bed, still wearing her nightie and ran downstairs and into the garden carrying her crayons and drawing book. The mulberry bush leaves were a glossy green, and next to Jack's grave Maud found some tiny white feathers. Maud sat down on the grass beside Jack's grave and stroked the earth that felt warm and soft. She opened her drawing book and drew a little red and blue hammock with Jack and her inside it. She smiled, and silently thanked Jack for visiting her in her dream. She knew that she could always return to this spot in their garden when she wanted to talk to him and keep filling up her drawing book with pictures of Jack.

What can I do to help?

Dr Alan Peterson offers a few coping strategies which can help children as they struggle with emotions, dreams, and questions about death. These include gathering further support, creating a ritual to honour the loss, encouraging creative expression, and discussing your next steps as a family.

Questions to ask

What would you like to do to honour the loss of your special pet? (Offer some suggestions like planting a tree, writing a message and turn this into a small headstone, make a memory bracelet to wear).

Key messages

- **The denial message:** We can get another pet for you.
- **The resilient message:** Your relationship with your pet was so special, what were the best things about this? Your tone when saying this must be one of curiosity.

Classroom activity

Appetizer: Memory stones

This is a symbolic exercise for a child to do and does require a bit of prep. Invite the child to go out into the school grounds (or their home garden) and collect up to ten stones. Give them a small plastic container, like a lunch box to hold the stones. Explain that they are going to decorate these. Once they have all the stones in the box, you can sit down with them for 10–15 minutes and encourage them to decorate the stones with crafting materials. I have known some children cover the stones in glue and then wrap the stones in coloured tissue paper. This can be seen as the children's way of protecting their memories. If they want to add messages to the stones, have some small pieces of card available for them to write their message on and keep this with the stones in the plastic container. I recommend keeping the plastic container in the classroom so that you have the option of offering this appetizer exercise to the children at another point, should they need to do further work.

Main course: The 'shared text' exercise

The story is projected onto a screen and the teacher and class read and analyse the story together, page by page. The children are directed to think about: identifying the character, the problem, the solution and the 'lesson learned'.

The teacher sets the scene to allow the children to engage their emotions and thoughts so that they can do more than just perform, we want them to engage their imaginations and begin to connect these to their feelings and personal circumstances, and to be able to give what R. Mead (2017, 'Two schools of thought: Success Academy's quest to combine rigid discipline with a progressive curriculum', *The New Yorker*, New York), calls, 'personally inflected interpretations' of the story. For example, if a character feels lonely, the children must get the message from the teacher that it is OK to explore beyond the surface meaning of the words in the story.

The day before the reading, the teacher prepares the children by inviting them to bring a picture of their pet into school. They then have the choice as to whether they link the story to their own relationship with their pet.

After you have completed reading the story, invite the children to draw a picture of how they remember their pet. This will be their memento from this exercise and something they can refer back to and hold onto.

If you don't have time to do the shared text exercise, what you can also do is read this story to a child, one-on-one, and follow this up by using the drilling technique and reflecting back what the child is saying to you until you get that Aha moment. You will recognize when you have reached this moment because the child will affirm this for you, as the child in my case did. Trust the process! You could do this in 10–15 minutes. The title, Come into the garden Maud was inspired by the Tennyson poem of the same title.

* * * * * * * * * * * * * * * * * * * *

Clinginess after the death of a parent

Reuben was 6 years of age when he was referred to me by his primary school SENCO. She was concerned that he could be very quiet, tearful, clingy and withdrawn. There had been angry outbursts at home (kicking and punching doors), and Reuben's teacher believed that the recent loss of his Mother was the cause of these behaviours. She hoped that as a result of his sessions, Reuben would be able to talk about his anxieties and learn some strategies to express his thoughts. After 12 sessions, these hoped for outcomes were achieved.

Understanding bereavement as trauma

Whenever a child or adult is faced with traumatic life events, particularly the loss of a loved one, the ability to survive the emotional and physical pain associated with the event will be influenced by the individual's level of personal resilience. (Bunce and Rickards, 2004, p. 1). Factors associated with resilience include secure attachments to significant others, absence of early loss and trauma, high self-esteem, social empathy, and an easy temperament. Reuben's attachment style had been disrupted through the loss of his Mother. The family's reduced level of resilience provoked attachment-seeking behaviours by him, which were misunderstood by stressed relatives. Fisher shows us the impact of trauma on the brain, and how many symptoms develop as a result. Through using the projected play mediums in the Play Therapy toolkit (painting, drawing, clay, sand and music), Reuben accessed his 'Noticing Brain', and gained greater awareness of his thoughts, emotions and sensations.

Separation and loss

Klein says (Bowlby, 1993, p. 93), 'every advance in the process of mourning results in a deepening in the individual's relation to his inner objects'. Reuben had a break-through while making a picture of his Dad. He sat silently with his head down for a few minutes, and then said, 'I want to make my Daddy happy.' This was something which was missing from his relationship with his Dad, so the fact that Reuben felt ready and able to tell me this directly was a sign of his trust in me and the way he was connecting to his feelings. He was expressing his deepest wish. We sat together, bearing what he found so difficult.

What a bereaved child goes through

Furman (1974, p. 163) says that the bereaved child has a threefold task – to cope with the immediate impact of the circumstances, to mourn, and to resume and continue his emotional life in harmony with his level of maturity. None of these tasks is completed within a prescribed timeframe. Bereavement has no clock. Depending on internal and external factors, each task may present ongoing difficulties for the bereaved or it may be resolved in such a way as not to impede functioning in later years.

A new pattern emerges

Reuben created a series of objects to represent his loss using the mediums of cutting, and imprinting new shapes, which represented the creation of new bonds, all of which symbolized a new stage in his grief process. The new shapes represented his growth in being ready to connect with other nurturing figures in his life.

First he a sequence of paintings. Before they had dried he cut them out with scissors and imprinted tissue paper onto the wet paintings that covered the painted image. Each stage of this process felt like a huge step emotionally. As he painted the tissue paper, he gave instructions out loud, 'Now we paint this, and now we press it down like this.' There was tremendous energy and strength in the way his body moved during the cutting out and pressing down – he stood at the table (he usually sat), and used his body weight to lean on the table as he pressed down on the tissue paper.

I felt he was creating a new pattern, and felt completely in synch with him as we created these imprints side by side. Each step in the painting process was symbolic of him creating stronger resilience for himself. He chose purple tissue paper which is a colour associated with spirituality and resurrection (Malchiodi, 2007, p. 156). He put his painting and mine into his special box symbolically including me in this new stage of trust and attachment.

The second object was a bracelet made out of a powder blue-coloured pipe cleaner. He used scissors to cut the pipe cleaner into thirds, and then secured the ends together by twisting them until he had formed a new shape, a circle with twisted knots securing the bracelet together. The knots weren't tight, just loose enough for him to slip the bracelet onto his wrist. Again, I felt the significance of this new shape, the broken, cut circle, similar to the new family he had, with his Mother cut out of the picture through death.

He explored this theme further in the sand. He put a crane into the sand and pulled on the winding cord. When the chord broke, he remained calm, and tried to make the crane work without the cord, but gave up quickly trying to make this work when he realized that with the broken cord, the attachment of objects to the crane was different, and difficult. He noticed this, and I remarked on this. Soon afterwards, he pushed the chord mechanism in with the broken cord, and moved on to drumming and banged the drum loudly. This can happen when a child has connected with their feelings and making a sound with a musical instrument allows them to release the energy that might have been bound up with that emotion. Immediately, the symbolism of the broken cord echoed loudly for me with the broken symbiosis Reuben suffered through his Mother's death.

After Reuben completed his play therapy his teacher told me his concentration had improved to the point where he could sit for longer periods of time at his desk and complete his work. This was a huge win for Reuben! He was able to settle down at his desk because he had found a settlement within himself. The objects he had created in his sessions, although not a replacement for his Mother, were somewhere for him to project his feelings of loss and begin to find a way to cope with his grief. When the child sees the external objectification of their feeling they feel freer because they are no longer having to contain this feeling themselves.

Bereavement usually affects a whole family. Any loss resonates with previous losses, which are often reawakened. Where grief is not acknowledged it can damage family relations in a number of ways. The anger of grief may be displaced onto a family member ('scapegoat') who becomes the target of all wrath. This happened in Reuben's case where he was blamed for showing his grief. His Dad found this especially difficult to see because he just wanted to move on from his loss and was angry with Reuben for not being able to do the same. This was damaging to the parent/child relationship in a number of ways. The trust between Father and son became fragile: Reuben didn't understand why his Dad was so angry with him and this only made things worse between them. Communication became fraught as his Dad shouted at him to stop being so difficult. Reuben didn't understand what he was doing wrong so he became particularly clingy with his Dad, seeking his approval which he rarely got. The one thing Reuben's Dad wanted Reuben to do was to stop showing him his grief. Reuben was expressing his grief in the only way he knew how. Sadly, although the play therapy gave Reuben a safe space to express his emotions, his parents were unable to cope with their own grief and create a safe space for Reuben at home, so the family dynamic of anger continued.

Allowing a family to witness emotional distress in one member can release them to talk about their own feelings (Hospice Education Institute, Online).

What do these children need? They need to hear the word 'dead,' and they need to hear in a gentle quiet way that their parent is not coming back, although we can understand why they would like that to happen. It was not Daddy or Mummy's choice. A simple explanation of what happened is appropriate; for example, Daddy was sick and sometimes the doctors can't fix the problem. Focusing on words and asking how they feel may be very frustrating for the surviving parent because they may not reach their child in this way. They need to focus on hugs, respecting their child's wish not to be left alone, their child's need to know where their surviving parent is, and how they can be found if they leave for a bit. Drawing pictures together, trying to replicate some of what Mummy or Daddy did with and for their child helps. Their child needs to feel cared about, and safe.

Story 2.4 The gate that never closes

Elsa was 8 years old when she found out her Mum was dying. She knew something was wrong because suddenly her Mum was out of breath and didn't want to take her daily walk with Elsa. Elsa loved these walks with her Mum, it was where she talked about her day and confided in her Mum about her worries. Her Mum listened carefully to Elsa and they usually had a picnic behind their favourite rock. Her Dad carried the picnic basket and laid out the blanket for the three of them to sit on. The high grasses surrounding the rock gave them some privacy and Elsa felt comforted that her Mum had found this safe place for them to be together.

When Elsa was young, she had snuggled next to her Mum as she slept and felt safe and secure inside her arms. Elsa felt her Mum's heartbeat which helped her to drift off to sleep feeling all was right with her world. In the morning her Mum would wake Elsa up by stroking her soft ears and the first thing Elsa saw after opening her eyes was her Mum's smile. Elsa felt like the luckiest girl in the world.

When she could walk properly her Mum had shown her where the best places were to play and introduced her to games that made Elsa happy. They played softball together and Elsa loved retrieving the ball her Mum had thrown for her. Elsa was full of questions and relied on her Mum's guidance and couldn't imagine never having this.

'Will the stars come out tonight?' Elsa asked

'Yes, they will,' said her Mum.

'How can you be so sure?' said Elsa.

'Nothing can stop the stars shining at night,' said Elsa's Mum.

When the stars appeared in the sky that night, Elsa smiled at her Mum and felt secure in her love.

Eventually, Elsa's Mum had to go to hospital to be looked after but the doctors said they had done everything they could do and sadly, Elsa's Mum was going to die. They told her she only had a few days to live.

Elsa sat quietly beside her Mum's hospital bed, her Dad sat on the other side looking very concerned.

Elsa could feel her heart beating very fast as she realized that soon her Mum would not be with them anymore. She felt scared and sad so climbed onto her Mum's bed and snuggled beside her. Elsa's Mum opened her eyes and smiled, as she always had at Elsa. This time Elsa saw tears in her Mum's eyes.

'I'm sorry little one,' her Mum said, and Elsa wiped the tears from her eyes.

'I know Mamma,' she said, 'I want to come with you,' Elsa said, her voice and heart breaking.

Elsa's Mum looked over at her Dad, 'I have a little something in my bag for Elsa, can you get it for me please?' Elsa's Dad went to her bag and found a matchstick size silver box. He passed it to Elsa. Elsa held it in her hands and read the message on the front of the box:

> This is a special gift
> That you can never see
> The reason it's so special
> It's just for you from me.
> Whenever you are lonely
> Or ever feeling blue
> You only have to hold this gift
> And know I think of you.
> You never can unwrap it
> Please leave the ribbon tied
> Just hold this box close to you
> It's filled with love inside.
> (Anon)

When she had finished reading, Elsa put her arms around her Mum's waist and sobbed.

'Oh Mamma, what will I do without you?' she said.

Elsa's Mum held her tightly. 'Know that you will always feel my love Elsa. And when you feel scared or lonely, hold your silver box.'

Elsa's Mum fell asleep quickly; the medication was powerful and stopped her from feeling any pain.

'We must be grateful for that,' said Elsa's Dad quietly.

Elsa wished with all her heart that her Mamma didn't need that medication and clung to her tightly as she slept.

Then a strange thing happened. Elsa could hear her Mum's breathing getting distressed; it was up and down and she was making little noises. Elsa kept her eyes closed and concentrated on her own breathing. At first it felt fast as her heart was beating so fast, then suddenly, her breathing started to slow down, Elsa counted in between breaths, five on the in five on the out, she kept repeating this until she heard her Mum's noises stop. There was a peaceful silence in the room as the two breaths sounded like one.

Elsa drifted into a dreamlike sleep, and in her mind's eye, Elsa saw herself approaching a garden gate. She recognized it. It looked friendly and there were flowers around it. The gate was open and the path forward was long and empty, as if it was waiting for someone to appear. Elsa turned around and saw her Mum walking towards her. As she reached Elsa she took her hand and squeezed it. Elsa felt the familiar warmth in her Mamma's touch and squeezed back. Elsa knew that this was the moment she had to say goodbye to her Mamma. She could not go through the gate with her, the gate was only open one way, and her Mamma's time had arrived, she was meant to go through it alone. Elsa felt a surge of energy surround her that felt just like the soft blanket her Mamma wrapped around her when she was cold. This was the hardest thing she would ever do, let her Mamma go. She knew that her Mamma would never let her go.

'It's Ok Mamma, I will be OK,' Elsa said.

Her Mamma smiled at her and Elsa could see her Mamma was fading fast, as her physical body was fading.

Her grip loosened on Elsa's hand and Elsa gently and slowly withdrew hers and took a step back from the gate.

Her Mamma turned around and smiled at Elsa, the same smile she always had and then she was gone.

When Elsa woke up she looked up at her Mamma. Her eyes were closed and she looked at peace. Elsa looked at her Dad who was holding her Mamma's hand and crying softly.

'She's gone Elsa, Mamma has gone.'

'I know,' said Elsa and kissed her Mamma's forehead.

'Goodbye Mamma,' she said to herself.

After her Mamma's funeral, Elsa told her Dad the story of her dream.

'I am so proud of you Elsa, you gave Mamma such a gift in letting her go, and I know how hard that must have been for you,' he said.

Elsa thought about all the wonderful things her Mamma had given her and said, 'It was, but I couldn't bear to see Mamma struggling to leave me,' she said.

'You have a heart as big and as wide as the sky,' said her Dad, 'and I love you.' Elsa hugged her Dad and together they held each other, and that night they watched the stars come out.

In her memory, they planted a mulberry tree in their garden behind their garden gate and Elsa visited this when she was feeling lonely and held her silver box. She'd sit next to the tree and tell her Mamma about her day. Every day Elsa looked at the gate and understood why it opened just one way.

What can I do to help?

Keep a watchful eye on children who have been bereaved of a parent because their grieving maybe unpredictable. Pay attention to signs such as deteriorating concentration of school work, deflective behaviour, tiredness and irritability. These are all signs of grieving.

Questions to ask

- Would you like to read a story with me?
- Would you like to make something to remember you Mum or Dad?

Key messages

- **The denial message:** Mummy will be thinking about you.
- **The resilient message:** It's OK to be sad about Mummy never coming back.

Classroom activity

Appetizer: Making a memory bracelet

These can be made out of raffia or pipe cleaners. The advantage of using raffia is that it has numerous strands which children like to gather together and pull apart until they are happy with the arrangement. The way they play with and organize the raffia into a bracelet usually reflects their level of comfort with their loss. You may need to help them with this and remind them that they are making it as a memory of their loved one. It doesn't have to be perfect, it can be exactly as they want it to be. That means that all the strands don't have to be the same length when they are tied together – all of this is significant in terms of what is says about the child's psyche. You don't need to analyse this, only to note it. The most important part about this exercise is to support the child to create the memory bracelet in the way that they want to. When they have finished making the bracelet don't be surprised if they want to give this to you. My advice is to decline this offer and encourage them to keep it by reminding them that they have made a special gift for their loved one. This helps the child to start to come to terms with their loss by owning their feelings associated with that loss.

Main course: Making a memory box

You will need a small box for this exercise, the size of a large matchstick box. Obviously take the matches out before giving this to the child! I keep a collection of these in my practice so I always have them to hand. A couple of sheets of shiny paper, silver and gold, as this is going to be a precious box. Invite them to choose a sheet and then wrap up the box in the paper and seal is at both ends so that it is covered and secure. A fine point black pen and some paper. Invite the child to write their special message to their parent on the paper and then cut this out for them and ask them to stick this onto their box.

This is a very powerful exercise to do as the child is literally formulating some of their feelings about their parent. Encourage them to keep this box with them and to hold it when they feel sad or lonely.

* * * * * * * * * * * * * * * * * * * *

Feeling different: where do I fit in?

Dylan was 7 years of age when he was referred to me by the local authority social worker. Dylan had been adopted when he was 5 years of age by a couple who had no children. Prior to that, Dylan had been in foster care since birth.

This case was a difficult one for the school because whatever resource they put in place to support Dylan, there were numerous triggers throughout his day that they could not prevent, for example, someone pushing in front of Dylan in the lunch queue. The school did a great job of supporting Dylan, but what they couldn't do was give Dylan the time and space that he needed to express his feelings through play therapy.

For adopted children who may struggle with the meaning of being adopted, and may experience feelings of loss and sadness, primary school is a difficult place to be because it has numerous opportunities for the child to be triggered. Mother's Day is a good example. He or she may wonder what was wrong with him or her; why did the birth mother place him or her up for adoption? The child may feel abandoned and angry. It is normal to see aggression, angry behaviour, withdrawal or sadness and self-image problems among adopted children at this age. The child attempts to reformulate the parts of his or her story that are hard to understand and to compensate for emotions that are painful. As a result, daydreaming is very common among adopted children who are working through complex identity issues.

A child may believe that he or she has had no control over losing one family and being placed with another. The child may need to have reassurance about day to day activities or may require repeated explanations about simple changes in the family's routine. Transitions may be particularly difficult. The child may have an outright fear of abandonment, difficulty falling asleep and, even, kidnapping nightmares.

It is helpful to understand how much of the child's life story has been explained to them; do they know the circumstances of their adoption and why their birth parents placed them up for adoption? If this information is not available to the teacher, their patience and understanding are crucial at this point. Parents may be pro-active by educating school personnel about the natural grieving issues related to adoption that their child is experiencing.

So when Dylan started his play therapy he had already experienced living in three different homes and understandably, had developed some difficulty with change. The smallest change in his routine could trigger a full-on emotional meltdown, and his adoptive parents were looking for new strategies to help Dylan. I explained to them at the outset that this process would take time for Dylan to discover his own strategies and that I would not be giving these to him because my job was to help Dylan discover his own.

This was the work we would explore together in the play room each week. From his first session Dylan presented as very anxious, standing still in the middle of the room while he orientated himself into yet another new surrounding. He didn't speak very much in his early sessions, but once we had established a trust and rapport, Dylan's story started to unfold.

After several sessions, Dylan walked over to the sand tray on the table and dug both his hands into the sand searching for the bottom. Dylan moved his hands about slowly, sifting the sand through his fingers. Dylan was especially drawn to three different houses and each week placed these in the same position in the sand tray: the big house at the top of the sand tray, a small sized house below that and the third house which was a tiny box house below that. I sat next to Dylan and noticed how carefully he placed these houses in the sand. It seemed important to him to have the houses almost on top of one another. Until one day, in addition to the three houses, Dylan placed the figure of a small boy in the sand. The boy stood facing the large house. He did not try and go into the house. After a few minutes of Dylan picked up the boy and knocked the big house over.

'He can't get into the house,' said Dylan, 'because the door is closed, it's always closed.' Dylan sounded sad and afterwards we talked about how Dylan missed his 'real home' where he felt the door was open. The session left a big impression on me and I thought about the boy with the closed door for several days because it reminded me of how the concept of a home has so many different meanings and how this made Dylan feel that he was different from his peers.

The following week Dylan's parents came to see me for their review and his adopted Mum said that for the first time Dylan had talked about his 'real home' and how much he missed it. He had cried in her arms for the first time.

'Dylan told me about the houses he has in the sand,' she said. I smiled at her.

'I'm so pleased to hear that Dylan has shared that story with you,' I said.

'Oh yes,' said Dylan's dad, 'he talks about it quite a lot now, and about the closed door too, which we now understand represents his birth home,' he said. 'For the first time yesterday, Dylan told his teacher about the door and how it upset him to think about the door to his birth home being closed. His teacher suggested that Dylan make a little clay model of his birth home and put a little door in it that opened,' he said.

'Dylan loves it,' said his Mum. 'He brought it home with him yesterday and has it in his room. Every night after we have read a story, we say goodnight to the clay house,' she said.

I was impressed. This family had embraced Dylan with open hearts and allowed him to express his sadness and grief at losing his birth Mum and birth home.

'How is his concentration now at school?' I asked.

'Oh, that's the best part,' said his Mum. 'Now, he is listening better and his teacher says that he doesn't stare out of the window as much. I feel like we have had a big breakthrough, thank you so much for helping Dylan,' she said.

'Thank you for trusting me with Dylan,' I said.

At Dylan's final session with me he arrived carrying his clay house.

'I wanted to show you my house,' Dylan said, 'and to tell you that now my door isn't closed anymore,' he said.

I think Dylan's struggle is quite common with adopted children who are constantly searching for what they call their 'real home'. In Dylan's case, once he had expressed his nightmare of being shut out, he was then able to find his own open door.

Adopted children feel different from their peers, as if they don't belong, and can struggle with fitting in and finding their place at school, which can cause them anxiety and stress. One way of helping to support these children is to read them the following story. This should give them a framework to start expressing their feelings in the safety of the one-to-one relationship with their teacher or learning assistant.

Story 2.5 Tilly Tea Pot

In this story Tilly feels a loss of self-esteem for looking different from the other tea pots. Adopted children can sometimes struggle with their self-esteem because they struggle with the concept of the 'real parent and 'real home', as in birth parent and birth home.

Tilly Tea Pot is put on the scrap heap because her spout is crinkly.

Tilly was born at a Pot factory called Pots R Us. She came out of the red Kiln with her beautiful crinkly spout, and was labelled 'different'.

Tilly feels lonely sitting all by herself on the scrap heap table. She watches all the other pots come out of the Kiln. None of the other pots have a crinkly spout. She wonders why she is the only one.

All the other pots sit together on a separate table waiting to be painted. Seeing Tilly standing alone puzzles them. They don't know what to say to Tilly. She looks different from them.

Dotty Paintbrush arrives and starts to give the other pots their special marks. Some get dots and others get stripes painted onto their lids and spouts. Tilly likes the colours of the dots and stripes – blue, red, yellow and pink glitter! She wonders what she has to do to have her crinkly spout painted with that pink glitter. She feels very sad to be missing out on the dots and the stripes.

The sugar bowls and other T. Pots start rattling their lids. Tilly thinks they are laughing at her. She feels doubly sad, and her spout starts to wilt. Instead of joining in, Tilly sits very quietly and still. She wants to shout at them and tell them that she is just like them really, but they are making so much noise Tilly's afraid they won't hear her small voice.

When Mr Box marches in with his lid open carrying a big roll of cellotape Tilly's worst fears look like they will come true.

Tilly knows what Mr Box is for. Mr Box will carry the T set to the Post Office, so it can be posted to a customer who has bought it! Tilly knows she won't be going with the T set, and she wonders where she will be going, and who her friends will be.

The other pots stop rattling their lids. They notice that Tilly is not going with them and Mr Box. They all move out of their huddle and stand in a line facing Tilly. Tilly moves closer to the edge of her table. A lone tear slides down her spout.

Tilly catches the eye of Billy, the milk jug. Billy lifts his spout slowly and waves at Tilly.

Tilly winks her crinkly spout at him. Billy realizes that Tilly wants to be friends with him, and understands that she's not sitting alone because she doesn't like him. He moves to the edge of the table and stands up for Tilly.

'I thought we were called Pots R Us,' yells Billy at the Kiln. Billy is the leader of the pot gang, and all the other pots listen to him.

The Kiln frowns his fire at Billy.

'If Tilly isn't coming with us and Mr Box, then our name is a lie. I thought we were all in this together,' shouts Billy wagging his spout.

All the other pots jiggle their lids in agreement.

The Kiln opens his door to find out what the noise is about. He's not used to being questioned.

'What's all this racket about in here?' bellows the Kiln.

Billy opens his spout and says:

'We are upset because Tilly isn't joining our T set,' says Billy. 'We want to know why Tilly has a crinkly spout and we don't?'

The Kiln opens his door a little further, and turns down his heat.

Tilly is quietly jumping up and down with joy. She's happy that the other pots want her to join them. So they do like her after all! Tilly looks down at her crinkles. They really are very pretty. When she looks up she notices something for the first time. Billy's stripes are wonky. Then she looks at Thelma and sees she's a square saucer! And her dots are multi-coloured instead of just black and white. Tilly looks at her crinkles again. Tucked inside she can see a few multi-coloured dots!

Tilly suddenly feels brave and excited.

Tilly moves closer to the edge of the table and finds the voice that she has been so nervous and scared of using.

'I am a crinkly pot,' Tilly says. 'You made me perfect just the way I am because I can pour in several directions not just one!'

All the other pots rush towards Tilly smiling and cheering.

'I'm a lucky lid,' says Violet.

'I'm a square saucer,' says Thelma.

The Kiln's eyes get wider and wider in disbelief. 'So you don't all mind being a bit different?' he asks.

All the pots including Tilly start rattling their lids and tipping their spouts. The cups swivel on their saucers.

'No, we love it,' they all cheer together.

'When I look at Thelma's pink cheeks I want to sing and dance,' laughs Tilly.

'And when I look at Tilly's crinkly spout I want to smile,' said Billy.

For the first time ever the Kiln smiles.

'Well, OK then,' he says. 'Let's put you together. Mr Box, please carry Tilly from the scrap heap to the despatch table.'

Tilly raises her crinkly spout and stops him.

'I want to join the T. set myself,' she says.

He moves aside so Tilly can pass. Tilly steps onto the table and joins the other pots. The pots cheer wildly! As Tilly steps over the gap between the two tables she notices that the gap is tiny. She had imagined that gap was wide, and is relieved to find out that it is not.

Tilly joins up the dots with the stripes and together they make a huge and colourful zigzag that dances around the shed. The Kiln lights up the factory shed with warm light, and the whole T. set assembles on a blanket to enjoy their own special T. party.

Tilly has finally come home.

Chapter 2

What can I do to help?

Questions to ask

- Where do you feel most comfortable?
- Have you ever felt like Tilly?

Key messages

- **The denial message:** Don't be silly, of course you fit in.
- **The resilient message:** I hear your discomfort. Would you like to tell me about this? Draw a picture of how this discomfort feels?

Classroom activity

Appetizer: A story in six parts

This is where you are going to use the 6PSM I referred to on page (44). This may appear like it's a long exercise but trust me, you can complete this in 10 minutes. Key to achieving that is to keep the child moving through the story; don't allow them to remain stuck in any box. If they are, just make a note of that for your own reference. Set the 10-minute timer.

You will need is a single sheet of white A3 paper. Divide this A3 paper into six boxes using a coloured pen chosen by the child. Their colour choice will give you some insight into their feelings. By inviting the child to choose the colour you are including them in the process and crucially, giving them a choice. For a lot of children this is where they start to learn how to cope with change. When they realize that they have a choice, they start to connect with their own voice and sense of empowerment. This is ultimately what will enable them to create and build emotional resilience. Number the boxes 1–6.

Six questions are always represented in fairy tales, and these are used as the story structure in 6PSM:

1. Who is (are) the main character/s (hero/heroine)?
2. What is the task or mission of the main character/s?
3. Who or what can help (if at all)?
4. What is the obstacle in the way or what prevents it from happening?
5. How does/do the main character/s cope with the obstacle?
6. What happens next or how does the story end?

You ask one question per box in chronological order and invite the children to draw their answer in each box. As the story continues and builds the children usually get completely absorbed in telling it, and their energy and movement changes. This is how you know they are making connections with their own story. When the story is finished, this is your opportunity to reflect on how the children are coping which will enable you to decide on the intervention possibilities.

Teachers will find this intervention a useful assessment tool to use prior to making a therapeutic referral. You may find that completing this tool is enough for the child. Lahad suggests asking yourself the following questions during this reflection:

- Does this story suggest an intervention that is balancing, helping the child to 'bounce back'? Is it about regaining strengths and separating from the teacher after a short and focused encounter?
- Does the story show very few coping resources, or too many channels in conflict? If so, then a longer therapy may be indicated.
- Does the story reveal developmental concerns and conflicts that belong to a very young age or are not at all age appropriate?
- Are the character's problems chronic, or is the quest circular, so that a supportive approach maybe the most suitable recommendation.

Main course: Four-part pizza

✻ ✻

Magical thinking after the death of a sibling

CASE STUDY 2.6

Harvey was 6 years old when he was referred to me by his primary school teacher for play therapy support following the death of his younger sister, Rachel. The school were concerned because Harvey was not his usual ebullient self, he was withdrawn and unusually quiet, and seemed to be struggling to accept his sister's death. His parents were married and lived together and were very concerned about Harvey's reaction to the loss of his sister, in addition to trying to deal with their own personal grief.

According to research done into sibling death, 5 to 8 per cent of children in the United States will experience the death of a sibling, but sadly the loss is rarely discussed, and siblings of terminally ill children are often overlooked (Fletcher, Mallick, Song and Wolfe, 2013, 'A sibling death in the family: Common and consequential', *Demography*, 50(3), 803–826.) This can have devastating consequences on the surviving children.

A recent study in *JAMA Paediatrics* followed all children in Denmark and Sweden from 1973 through to 2013. More than 55,000 of these children experienced the death of a sibling before they turned 18. In the 37 years of follow-up, these children were more than 70 per cent more likely to die as well. Although the overall risk of death remained low throughout these years, it was highest in the first year after a sibling's death. During that period, children who lost a sibling have a mortality rate two and a half times that of other children.

It is true that in this study, many of the children who died later died of the same disease as their sibling. However, another factor could be the emotional impact and its effects on mental health, especially in the short term and that emotional damage can linger. A study of young adults who lost siblings to cancer found that most still had not worked through their grief, even nine years later (J. Sveen, A. Eilegård, G. Steineck and U. Kreicbergs, 2014).

Poor social support was cited as the main reason they had not worked through their grief, which just underlines the need to help children to cope with feelings of loss and change.

In Harvey's case, his parents' struggle with their own grief affected the way they communicated with Harvey. His Mum told me during the assessment that whatever she offered Harvey he pushed her away, and it was clear that she was finding this very frustrating. Both Harvey's parents were academics and on their own admission, struggled to be 'touchy, feely'. I could see that they were approaching their grief as if it were a problem to be solved. I explained my concept of the backpack metaphor and how children needed help with unpacking their worries and they understood this.

Story 2.6 In a nutshell

When they were 5 years old Daphne and Davina joined a weekly ballet class, called The Nutcrackers, taught by their Mother's best friend who had also taught their mother. The dancing tradition between the families had continued and Daphne and Davina's parents were thrilled by this, attended all their dancing competitions and shows. Of the two sisters, Daphne was the most graceful; her pirouettes dazzled and Davina was happy to stand back and watch her sister. When their feet were covered in red blisters they would rub one another's feet and if one forgot their steps the other would literally step in and show the other the way forward. Davina felt safe when Daphne was around, her world felt complete, she felt she could conquer and overcome any obstacle because Daphne was good at being the leader – 'let's dance!' she would announce at Christmas after they had opened their presents, her solution for everything, awkward silences, sad moments and any celebration. Davina managed to scoop up all the feelings in the room and express these through her pointed toes. Their Christmas treat from their parents was to watch *The Nutracker* ballet performed at the Opera House in London.

Losing Daphne was something her twin sister never imagined she would have to do.

Their Mother loved to tell them their birth story, how they had grown in her womb together and how on their sonograms she could see them holding hands. Daphne and Davina were born on a bright Monday morning, and Daphne had died, on a dull Monday evening, as if her life had opened with a smile and ended with a shower of tears in the form of rain.

Their mother encouraged Davina to be herself, to shine just as she was, but Davina always felt happier when Daphne was the one shining and she could bask in her light. The light felt warm and soft and comforting. Now Davina's world was overshadowed by Daphne's death, and she wasn't sure if she would ever feel light again.

Davina found that she didn't want to dance anymore without Daphne and so she retreated into her books. She missed their shared language, never having to explain anything to each other. Now everything felt like a big effort and Davina felt tired and lonely.

Davina and Daphne were obsessed with the dolls in *The Nutcracker*, how they were magically brought to life and performed their dance. At home they had made replica dolls, stitched and sewn their tutus out of pink satin and staged their own version in their bedroom.

'Ta-dah'! they cried in triumphant unison as the dolls danced around their bedroom.

As Christmas approached, their mother told Davina she had tickets for them to see *The Nutcracker* performance on stage at The Royal Opera House! For the first time Davina felt a flicker of excitement! Maybe, just maybe if she went to the opera, she would find Daphne sitting next to her … she badly want to see her again, to hear her voice, which made Davina feel happy and loved.

At the Opera House Davina took her seat next to her parents. Her Mum put her arms around her and kissed the top of her head.

'I hope you enjoy this, my love,' she said.

Daphne sat quietly hoping that the empty seat beside her would suddenly be filled by Davina. When a lady sat down in the seat Daphne looked shocked to see her. What was this woman doing in Davina's seat?! She felt the urge to tell her to move but she was scared she would get into trouble from her Mum, so instead, she kept her eyes on the stage, her heart was racing and her throat felt tight from holding back her tears. Daphne wasn't coming to the opera.

At the end of opera when people started leaving their seats, Davina slowly turned her head towards the lady next to her. She smiled at Davina and looked quite friendly. She had green eyes, just like Daphne's. Davina did a double take and looked straight into the woman's eyes, feeling her heart race as she did.

'Wasn't that a fantastic show?' the lady said.

Davina could only nod in reply, she felt oddly comforted by this lady and she didn't know why. After the lady said goodbye to Davina, she stood up and left her seat. Davina looked at the empty seat and saw a small white feather on the chair. Davina picked it up and it felt soft and smooth to her touch. She instinctively held the feather close to her heart and sat quietly while the opera house emptied.

When they got home, Davina went upstairs to her bedroom and sat in front of her mirror. She placed the feather on her dressing table and looked at her familiar face in the mirror. She saw Daphne staring back at her and she smiled. She felt a familiar warmth. Going to *The Nutcracker* alone would never be the same as Davina realized that she carried Daphne in her heart.

What can I do to help?

- Assign a buddy to the child in school.
- Start a bereavement group at school with creative activities (see suggestions at the back of this book).
- Create a check-in system with the child. See appendices for the check-in exercise.

Questions to ask

- In what ways do you identify with Davina?
- Are there any shared interests that you did with your sibling that you would like to carry on with?

- **The denial message:** You have plenty of other friends; try not to get so upset.
- **The resilient message:** In what way would you like to maintain contact with your friend?

Classroom activity

Appetizer: Object relations

This is a narrative-based exercise and good to do with a child who is talkative. Even if they are not, it can help to draw them out of their shyness.

Set up from your toolkit box a small selection of miniature figures. I like to have up to ten figures, with a mixture of humans, animals and houses. Try and at least get two adult figures, one male, one female, and small children, that represent a family unit. Animals can be a dog, cat, pig, tortoise, turtle and lion.

Invite the child to select one object from the table and then to hold that object in her hands for a minute. While she is doing this, sit next to her and be quiet. If she looks unsure and keeps looking at you for guidance, encourage her to look at her object and say:

'I wonder who this is that you have chosen? Would you like to tell me about him/her?' This gives the child permission to focus on her object and to start to connect with this. What you want is for the child to transfer her feelings onto the object and to tell you her story through the object.

This is an extremely effective exercise to do with both children and adults. I have seen adults quickly shift from their adult self into their child self and be able to access stories that have been tucked away in their broken hearts. The use of the object gives them and the child, 'safe distance' from which to explore and openly talk about their feelings.

When the child is talking, stay with whatever they are saying, don't interrupt them and try to analyse what they are saying. This is where you will be using your reflective skills to good effect! Simply reflect back what the child is telling you which will give them space to offload. Stay curious about the object's character: where are they from, where do they live, what are they interested in, what concerns them. These are all questions you can ask at the appropriate point especially if the child gets a bit stuck or, doesn't know how to start her story. The child will be talking about herself so this information will be really useful for you to hear.

When the 10 minutes is up, tell the child that it's time to say goodbye to her object. Allow her time to accept that and let her say farewell and place the object back on the table. This act in itself maybe the first time the child has been able to exercise choice and her voice in the matter of saying goodbye.

After the exercise has finished make some notes and perhaps discuss these with one of your colleagues or mentors. For sure there will be some insights in the child's story that may help you to support them moving forward.

Main course: Four-part pizza

* * * * * * * * * * * * * * * * * * * *

Separation anxiety caused by the loss of a friend through relocation

CASE STUDY 2.7

When I was 11 years of age I moved with my family from the UK to live in South Africa. My Dad's job was relocated and while this was a great career opportunity for him, it was a devastating move for me as I left my school friends and best friend behind. I can clearly remember our tearful goodbye; our parents had to prise us apart we were so distraught. This was in the 1970s long before the Internet made communicating instantly accessible, and we had to rely on letter writing and making cassette tape recordings for each other. I couldn't make telephone calls because it was too expensive, so waiting for the post to arrive each week (in those days a letter could take up to two weeks to arrive!) was both anxiety provoking and exciting for me, and often the only light that made me feel normal again: a connection with my best friend. I struggled to connect emotionally and culturally with my peers at school and learned to never underestimate the impact of moving to a different location, be it country or town, on a young child. It is a wrench for them as they leave familiar people and relationships behind to start all over again. It puts pressure on them to make new friends quickly whilst they are grieving the loss of leaving close friendships behind, as I did.

The effect of moving on children

One study in the *Journal of Social and Personality Psychology* documents how frequent moves disrupt a child's friendships, which can make this emotionally tough on them. For introverted children and those who struggle with anxiety, this can be especially trying. Teachers might see a child moping, crying, becoming inattentive or hyperactive and acting out – yelling, hitting, being defiant or stubborn. These are all red flags for adults to pay attention to their children's emotional state and to ask them how they are feeling, to take time out to connect with them. They are telling you that they are feeling stressed.

A child's hurts are expressed through being upset about small issues. A good example of this was a child in my practice whose Dad was in the military and had moved abroad as part of a work promotion. His wife and two young children remained at home so the children could finish their school year before moving abroad to join him. My client was 6 years old at the time of his move and really struggled with missing her Dad. If her Mum asked her if she was missing her Dad she would say no, and run off, but the truth was she was heartbroken and too overwhelmed to cry about losing him. It was too big a hurt for her to face head-on. But then her sister went into her dressing up box and tried on her angel dresses without asking her. The child burst into tears. That faint hint of a loss – what if her sister wouldn't give her dresses back? – triggers her feelings of deeper loss. She can just about bear to feel upset about the possible loss of her dressing up dresses, but she can't bear to focus on her Dad's absence.

Story 2.7 The Egg without a Shell

Ava and Zadie had been best friends since kindergarten. Now they were in primary school and their friendship had grown stronger with every year. They knew each other's favourite colours – Ava's was red, Zadie's was black – favourite foods – Ava's was chocolate chips, Zadie's was cake, but not just any cake, chocolate chip fudge cake! Ava called at Zadie's house every morning so they could walk to school together, barely pausing for breath as they caught up on their overnight news.

'Hi Z,' Ava said to Zadie as she opened her front door.

'Hi A,' Zadie replied smiling.

At school they ran the A to Z Girl Group, and at break time they organized playground plays. Ava came up with the ideas and Zadie was the stage manager, organizing who took which role and how during each play time break they could act out another scene. It was thrilling! So far they had staged, 'Zigzag' one of their plays during a school concert. Everyone cheered at the end and they ate plenty of cake.

Now Ava's life was about to be turned upside down. Her Mum and Dad told her that her Mum's job was relocating to another country and they would be moving to live in the United States of America. They wanted to know what Ava thought about this idea.

Ava was speechless. A new country, she thought to herself, I don't want to live in a new country thank you very much, I am happy living in this one.

'What about school, The A to Z Group, and Zadie! Yes, WHAT ABOUT ZADIE!' Ava cried.

'It's only for a year,' her Mum said, seeing Ava getting upset. 'We will have a big house and a pool, and you will make new friends,' she said, trying hard not to get upset herself. Her Dad put his arm around Ava to comfort her but Ava shrugged it off.

'But I like it just fine here,' Ava said, 'why can't I stay here and you and Daddy go and live in this new country?' Ava said. Her parents looked at each other.

'Well,' said her Dad slowly and gently, 'Zadie can come and visit us anytime,' he said. 'You could even decorate a spare bedroom for her, if you'd like to,' he said. He looked at his wife hoping this would encourage Ava, but it seemed to make things worse.

'I hate you, Mummy,' said Ava, 'you know how much fun we have in The A to Z Group and our next play is almost ready – The Egg without a

Shell – and now what will I do without that, without Zadie?' Ava shouted. 'Zadie IS my shell!' she screamed as she stood up, not waiting for her Mum to reply before she ran to her room. Her parents looked at each other. They would give Ava a few days to calm down and then revisit the subject with her.

When Ava told Zadie the next day, their walk to school was unusually quiet. Both girls walked with their heads down, their backpacks and boots felt very heavy, their hearts aching at the prospect of being apart from one another.

'I suppose we could text,' said Zadie.

'I know we can, but it's not the same as seeing you, is it?' Ava replied.

'Suppose not,' said Zadie.

At school their teacher noticed how quiet both girls were. They didn't skip back into class, in cahoots about something that had just happened in the playground, both talking at the same time yet seeming to understand each other perfectly well. Their friendship was the envy of other children. When one girl was upset, the other would be there to console her. They were each other's backup. They had matching school books, covered in the same designs, spare wallpaper from Zadie's Mum's decorating.

Their teacher noticed how quiet both girls were in class and struggled to finish their classwork. During one exercise which involved the class dressing up, Zadie burst into tears when one of her classmates took her favourite outfit from the dressing up box.

'That's mine and now I have nothing to wear,' she cried.

The teacher took Zadie to one side. 'You could try something else on Zadie, what about the blue dress?' she said.

'I don't want the blue dress, the red dress is the one I always wear and the blue one isn't the same,' she cried.

All Zadie could think about was the fact that Ava was leaving her and how lonely she felt thinking about that.

'Ava might be moving to a new country,' Zadie said.

'I see,' said her teacher. 'Well, that's a big deal for you isn't it because Ava is your best friend,' Zadie stopped crying and looked at her teacher.

'I don't want her to go,' she said.

Sometimes,' said their teacher, 'things happen to us that we can't control, and although it's hard to understand at the time, these things can often turn out to be full of new things that we quite like,' she said.

'Such as?' she said.

'Such as having different things to talk about and share with each other, such as visiting one another,' she said.

Zadie didn't look convinced. By this stage Ava had wandered over to find out why Zadie was upset.

'How about this? I know how you like making lists Zadie so I'd like you both to use these great skills and make a list of all the things you are going to miss about being separated, and when you've finished the list, bring it to me and then we will talk about phase two,' she said.

'Phase two?' Zadie said. 'What's phase two?'

'Aha, that's the fun bit,' the teacher said, 'that's where you get to be creative and come up with all the great ways in which you two can keep in contact with each other,' she said.

The girls' faces started to brighten up. Ava stood up, hitching her backpack onto her back. 'OK, come on Zadie, let's get started on the list,' Ava said.

The following day, the girls appeared at their teacher's table, and Ava held out a piece of paper with the heading written in red and black crayon: 'How the egg talked to the shell even though the shell was not in the same room.' She glanced down the list. There were two columns: one marked MISSING, the second marked FOUND. The girls had completed both phases of the exercise! They had big grins on their faces.

'Well done!' she praised them. 'I see you have been thoughtfully busy, and have found the solutions for YOUR PROB,' she said.

'Yes,' said Zadie, 'Ava is going to facetime me every day on her trip to school, which might be in the car, but that's OK, and I am going to see if we can set up a virtual group for The A to Z Group,' she said.

'And,' said Ava, 'my Dad has said that he will set up an email account for me so that Zadie and I can write each other whenever we feel like it, which will be a lot, right Zadie?' Ava said.

'Of course,' said Zadie, 'and I can email you pictures too!' Both girls looked ecstatic at the prospect of being in charge of all this high tech stuff.

'It's the beginning of our new Empire!' said Zadie.

'Yay!' said Ava, and they high-fived each other.

At pick up the next day, Ava's Mum thanked her teacher for all her help with solving the PROB as the family had come to call it. Even her Dad had said how impressed he was with their lists which were, of course, stuck up on the fridge as a reminder!

As the time approached for Ava's Mum to make her decision about whether to accept her new job offer in the new country, she asked Ava how she was feeling about this. It was a Friday evening and her Dad had made pizza for them all, Ava's favourite, with chilli.

'I'm cool, Mum,' Ava said. Her parents exchanged glances.

'I will miss Zadie, like MAD, and I wish she could come too, but we can still talk, like anytime, and I can't wait to decorate her bedroom in our new house!' Ava said.

'And that will be in …'

'Black, of course" said Ava smiling at her parents.

What can I do to help?

- Plan to help the child maintain the relationship with peers, using technology which has changed a lot and can be used to sustain distant relationships. If I had had access during my move it would have eased my loss and anxiety about making new friends.
- Actively listen to the child. This practice will give your child the space to express their feelings so that they feel heard by you. This helps to build trust and resilience.
- Suggest your child joins a friendship circle at school or, is connected with a buddy group.

> ## Questions to ask
>
> Which character in the story do you identify with and why? If the child struggles to answer this direct question, offer them a creative medium like drawing a picture of their struggle instead. You can then use this picture as a conversation prompt to learn more about their needs. Start your conversation with:
>
> 'I'm curious about X in your picture. Would you like to tell me about this?'

> ## Key messages
>
> - **The denial message:** Your friend had to leave with her family and that's that.
> - **The resilient message:** What are some of the best things about your friendship with X that you would like to remember?

Classroom activity

Appetizer

Make a memory bracelet exercise. Suggest that the child makes two bracelets, one for herself and the second for the child who has left. It's a nice idea to suggest that the child sends this bracelet to her friend or, if the child is still in school, consider getting the children together to do this exercise together.

Main course: Four-part pizza or Unpacking the backpack

* *

Separation anxiety through separation and divorce

Kyra, aged 8, started having play therapy after her Mum could no longer cope with her angry meltdowns, following her divorce from Kyra's Dad.

'I used to hear Mum and Dad arguing, and I used to yell at them to stop, but they didn't listen to me, and carried on. I ran up to my room and stayed there until they stopped,' she said.

'All I wanted was for them to agree and stop arguing with each other. I hated saying goodbye to my Dad at the end of our weekends together. Mum was never nice to him, and I felt sorry for him. Living with Mum in the house was not the same after Dad left,' she said.

'Mum kept telling me to stop worrying, that everything would be OK, but I felt so upset, no-one was listening to me.'

I've worked with many children of divorced parents and the one thing they have in common is a struggle to accept the loss of the family unit. While there may be good custody arrangements in place, the child still has to learn how to manage the transitions each time they leave one home to stay at the other. These are small losses for them to cope with emotionally and often get overlooked.

What complicates this loss for children is when the parents fight about the custody arrangements. Children like clear boundaries and routines, and when these are disrupted by difficult and controlling adult behaviours, the children are the ones who suffer the most because they usually don't have a place to express their feelings of anger, frustration and sadness about losing their family unit. It is important to give these children tools to help them process these losses.

In my practice, children of divorced parents respond well to play therapy because they have access to a safe and boundaried space that is theirs where they can play out their worries with a third person. The third person is important to them because very often they can't tell their parents how they are feeling because they are anxious about upsetting them; generally they believe it is their fault their parents have divorced.

Over half of couples divorcing in the UK in 2007 had at least one child aged under 16. This meant that there were over 110,000 children who were aged under 16 when their parents divorced; 20% of these children were under 5 years old. However, many more children go through parental separation each year that are not included in figures like this, as their parents were not married (The Royal College of Psychiatrists).

Children aged 5–7 have not developed the cognitive functioning to be able to verbally articulate their feelings directly to adults. Play and creative arts therapies give these children a space and the tools to express their feelings.

When parents no longer love each other and decide to live apart, a child can feel as if their world has been turned upside down. The level of upset the child feels can vary depending on how their parents separated, the age of the child, how much they understand, and the support they get from parents, family and friends.

In children up to the age of 9, their world is a dependent one, in which they rely on parents to meet their physical, psychological and emotional needs so when parents separate and divorce a child may feel:

A sense of loss – a child loses not only their home, but also their whole way of life, which is different and changed.

- Afraid of being left alone – if one parent leaves, perhaps the other parent will also leave.
- Angry at one or both parents for the breakdown of the relationship.
- Anxious about having caused the parental separation and breakdown: guilty.
- Rejected and insecure.
- Torn between both parents: disloyal.

These feelings can be made worse by the fact that many children have to leave their family home, and live somewhere else, as well as change their school. Most families separating will face some financial hardship, even if they did not experience money difficulties before. This can bring loss in the form of a child being unable to continue their extracurricular activities because the parent no longer has the spare money to afford them, or treats may disappear, so that there is no more going to the fair or cinema. These changes can cause emotional stress for the parent and the child which can have an impact on their relationship.

Even if the parental relationship had been tense or violent, children may still have mixed feelings about their parents' separation. The children I have seen in my practice have all held onto a wish that their parents get back together and the family unit is restored.

Emotional and behavioural problems

Children can become insecure when their parents separate because the separation may trigger how they express their attachment. If children have an insecure attachment style it is likely their behaviour will reflect that insecurity. Knowing about the different attachment styles can help teachers understand children who are struggling with separation issues and use strategies based on that attachment style. Refer to the attachment style list in Chapter 1.

Consequently the separation through divorce may cause children to regress to a younger age. A parent may therefore see bed-wetting, 'clinginess' nightmares, worries and general disobedience and dissent. Some of these behaviours may also show up at school and can be distressing for the child who is now 'standing out' in the classroom. This type of behaviour can happen before or after visits to the parent who is living apart from the family. These are red flags for teachers to note, maybe in a diary which they share with the parents, not to shame them, but to enable them to use as a point of offering some additional emotional and practical support at home. For the grieving child, some of these regressions will provoke feelings of shame as they lose their dignity and privacy and being different from their peers.

Story 2.8 Saul in the city

Saul hadn't eaten pancakes for a month. He was hungry for their comforting smell, the way his Mum made them.

Saul's parents were getting a divorce. His parents explained to him that they both loved him, and that wouldn't change.

But Saul felt confused. If they loved him, why couldn't they all live together? Saul felt sad and lonely. He sat at the kitchen table doing his homework, alone. In the family home, Saul had looked forward to the Friday night pancake making ritual with his Mum and Dad. Every Friday after school, he would help his Mum assemble the ingredients, crack the eggs into her mixer, and they would talk about the day's happenings – his dislike of spelling tests, her love of writing. His Dad would flip the pancakes in the pan, high in the air, so high Saul wondered if they would ever come down, but they always did, and his Dad would squeeze his special chocolate sauce over them.

'Say when,' his Dad said, holding the bottle upside down over the pancake.

'More, more,' shouted Saul, and they would burst into laughter.

Now, in the new arrangement, Saul lay in bed at his Dad's new house, staring up at the ceiling which was painted a plain white colour, worrying that his Dad might get fed up with him and leave, and then where would he stay on his Dad's nights? Saul struggled to get to sleep. He imagined that he could hear all the slugs crawling around outside in the garden, and the aeroplanes flying overhead. He hugged his teddy tightly.

The next day, when his Dad dropped him off at school, Saul clung to his legs crying. Saul's Dad bent down and hugged him, kissed him on his forehead, and said he would see him later. Saul had to be peeled off his Dad by his teacher. His Dad stood still, his heart heavy, waving goodbye to his son. He had never known his son be so clingy.

Saul's teacher tried to reassure his Dad that during his classes, Saul seemed quite happy and settled, but he got anxious just before home-time. She wondered if anything was wrong at home?

'Saul's Mum and I have separated,' he said, 'we are getting a divorce. Saul lives with me Monday to Wednesday at my new place, and with his Mum Thursday to Sunday in our old home. I have made a new bedroom for him at my place and I thought he liked it,' he said.

After school, Saul's Dad suggested they go for a walk in the park. They walked slowly beside each other.

Saul looked sad, pale faced and glum,

'What's the matter?' said his Dad,

'I miss my mum.'

'I'm just scared that my heart won't mend, because all I've got is you and Mum, in the end'.

Saul's Dad knelt down so he was facing his son, reached out and held both his hands.

A small tear ran down Saul's face.

'I've had an idea,' Saul's Dad said.

Saul looked brighter.

'This week, why don't you and I choose some paint for your bedroom at my house and …'

'Paint the sea horses!' said Saul

'Yes!' said his Dad, 'we can paint the sea horses.'

'And dolphins,' said Saul.

'And the dolphins,' said his Dad.

Saul hugged his Dad, then quickly pulled away, looked confused.

'But what about Mummy?' Saul said. 'She won't know about the new sea horses and Dolphins, will she?' he said.

'How about we invite Mummy over to my house after we have finished painting, so that she can see how happy they are?' he said.

Saul could see that his dad was trying. Things would never be the same, but they could be different.

Saul hugged his Dad tightly.

Maybe, just maybe, they would be all right.

The following week, Saul went to school and told his teacher about the new sea horses and dolphins on his ceiling at his Dad's house. He described how he had chosen the colours and how his Dad had painted the sea horses and Dolphins in great detail, and how he had given them all names.

'Now it doesn't matter which bed I'm sleeping in,' Saul said, 'I can say goodnight to Mummy and Daddy and the seahorses pass on the messages for me,' he said. His teacher smiled,

'That sounds like a very good solution, Saul,' she said.

She knelt down beside Saul and said, 'It's almost Friday, Saul, and I know how much you miss your pancake Friday night, so I've been wondering, what if you started a new ritual at Daddy's house on a Wednesday?' she said.

Saul looked thoughtful. He wasn't sure that he wanted two pancake nights.

'I don't know,' said Saul.

'What do you and your Dad like doing together?' she said.

'Football, checkers sometimes,' said Saul not sounding very enthusiastic.

'Let's find something that you have always wanted to do with Dad.' Saul's face suddenly lit up with excitement.

'Skateboarding!' shouted Saul. 'We watch a game on Wednesdays called, 'Get Your Skates On', and we have secret bets on who will win, but don't tell my Mum that,' Saul said.

His teacher smiled again.

His teacher could feel Saul's excitement at this prospect of having this special time with his Dad.

'Well, I think that sounds like a terrific idea Saul, shall we mention it to Dad at pick up time today?' Saul nodded enthusiastically.

'Wednesday will be called the new Friday,' he said looking pleased with himself.

At pick up time that day, Saul ran into his Dad's arms and told him about wanting to have, 'special time' with him on a skateboard. He was so excited he could barely explain what he meant, all his Dad saw was Saul's smiling face, which he hadn't seen in a long time. Whatever it was, Saul's Dad felt the answer was in a skateboard.

The following week Saul took a photograph of his new skateboard into school. He held this up proudly to show his teacher. In the photograph Saul and his Dad were standing next to the board which had been decorated by Saul, and was called Henry.

'Well done, Saul,' said his teacher.

'Thank you,' said Saul, 'I'm so happy Mummy and Daddy now get it.'

What can I do to help?

The most important thing you can do to help is to offer the child acceptance and acknowledgement. This helps them to cope better with any feelings of shame or embarrassment. The principle of accepting the child as is one of the principles of non-directive play therapy, founded by Virginia Axline in the 1960s. This is at the heart of my practice, and I have seen that the more this principle is extended to children who are struggling with their emotions, the more willing they are to be open and honest, because they feel safe from being judged whilst experiencing their personal shame. Whatever children are rejecting about their circumstances, they may be experiencing some guilt, so it is paramount that the teacher acknowledges these feelings and learns to separate them from his behaviour: acceptance does not imply approval.

A simple way of applying acceptance and acknowledgement in the classroom is to learn how to talk to children when they are responding emotionally, i.e. from the right side of their brain and not their left, where their rational thought is. For example, it is pointless telling a grieving child that it makes rational and practical sense for him to split his time between Mummy and Daddy's homes now that they are separated, when the child is crying and upset. At this point the child is reacting from the right side of his brain, where his emotions and feelings are. He won't be able to accept this rational reasoning. A good way of helping the child shift from the right to the left side of his brain is to read him a story in which he can identify his feelings. Through this identification, the child discovers ways of coping with his difficult feelings. After learning this he will be able to calm down and you will notice this because only then will he be able to start to hearing what the adult is suggesting. This point is reached when children can access the left side of their brain, where their rational thought is.

In my practice, I call this process unpacking the child's invisible back pack. Every child carries one, and when they first enter play therapy their back is heavy with their worries. I help them to unpack them, look at them and understand them.

In divorce cases, a child's trust in his dependence on his parents makes him feel they are now behaving in an undependable way, even though they have arranged for solid caretaking between them and are committed to those arrangements. The separation of the parents is a major transition for young children, and it's important for parents to react by re-establishing a sense of family connection by introducing the three R's: routine, ritual and reassurance. This makes children feel safe and helps to restore their sense of trust in security, familiarity and dependency. These three Rs can also be created at school to further support the child cope with this major change in their lives. For some children this consistency may be the only consistency they have, especially if their parents are at war with one another. As Robert

Emery, Professor of Psychology and Director of the Center for Children, Families, and the Law at the University of Virginia, says, 'pain is not pathology'. Grief is not a mental disorder. Children are entitled to their feelings and need time to be allowed to grieve this loss.

When parents explain that they have tried telling their children 'not to worry', I explain that in this transaction they are dismissing their child's feelings. Telling a child not to worry rarely stops the child worrying. It can make the situation worse for the child. Parents don't want to intentionally hurt their children and believe that by trying to stop them from worrying they are doing their job, when the point is, by acknowledging their child's feelings, they start to understand them and the child then feels heard.

This is definitely the moment to bring in the three As:

- *Acknowledge* the child's struggle: I hear that you are upset/angry/frustrated.
- *Accept* them where they are and what they are telling you about how they feel: it is OK to be upset/angry/frustrated.
- and take any further *Action* to support them process these feelings: what would be most helpful to you to express these difficult feelings? If the child does not know, this is the moment to offer them a creative resource. You should probably expect them not to know, which is fine, this is your cue to offer them a space to use a creative resource.

Note: if you move too quickly into the action stage before acknowledging the child's feelings or accepting them, the child will react by rebelling, which means their behaviour could get ramped up. If this happens, know that you are moving too quickly into finding a resolution. This is the time to contain them by simply acknowledging their feelings and telling them that you are going to spend with them alone to help them. Arrange this time the same day, if you can, and use that time to read them an appropriate story. Follow my instructions for 'how to use storytelling as a therapeutic tool with children' in Chapter 2. Don't be put off by the word 'therapeutic'. This section is not full of jargon! I have simplified this process for you so that you can do this exercise in 30 minutes.

Questions to ask

- Do you fantasize about your parents getting back together and you all living altogether again as a family?
- What special things would you like to do with your parents on a regular basis?
- What rituals do you miss doing with your parents?
- Who can you talk to when you are feeling sad/lonely/angry/frustrated?
- Do you have any friends in a similar situation?

Key messages

- **The denial message:** Maybe things will work out with Mummy and Daddy.
- **The resilient message:** You can still love Mummy and Daddy even though you don't all live together anymore.

Classroom activity

Appetizer: Design a game

This is a simple visualization game which involves asking the child to use their imagination and create their ideal game to use with their best friend, one which would give them both superpowers. To do this 10-minute game, give the child a large paper plate and some crayons. Tell them that this game is one which they can return to again and again and that this is just the start. The simple idea here is for you to start creating a dialogue with the child about their feelings. Invite them to sit down next to you at a small table and give them a paper plate. Take a plate yourself. You could start this game by telling them a quick story about a game you used as a child their age which will help to set the scene. I sometimes use this technique and it is a very effective scene setter and helps to contextualize things for the child so that they quickly access their imagination.

Start by saying: 'if you could design a game that would help you to change this upsetting situation, by giving you superpowers, what would it look like and what would those superpowers be?' and go from there. This is the equivalent of, 'Once Upon a Time.' You are helping the child to start.

Tell them to draw their game on the front of the paper plate. If they get into this, you could invite them to return to this the following week.

Main course: Unpacking the backpack

* * * * * * * * * * * * * * * * * *

Sleep disruptions following the death of a grandparent

Sleep disruption after the death of a loved one is a very common symptom of grief, in all age groups, from babies through to adolescence. The differentiating factor is that young children may be unable to connect sleep disruption to their loss and grief, so they need help to see that this is a normal reaction to losing a loved one. Doing so will minimize their fear and anxiety that something is wrong.

Children often long for others to recognize and acknowledge their pain, and the sleep disruption is their way of flagging this up.

Families differ in their closeness, hierarchy, proximity, relationships, and overall dynamics. With such differences, grandparent/grandchild relationships obviously run the spectrum from 'you-are-like-a-parent-to-me' type relationships to 'see-you-next-Christmas' type relationships.

Many grandchildren have very close relationships with their grandparents and rely on them for a number of their social, emotional, or physical needs. When a close grandparent dies, the grandchild often feels like they've lost someone akin to a parent which is intensely painful. They may have lost a favourite ritual and routine, and helping them to re-establish new ones will enable them to cope better with their loss.

I was fortunate to have close relationships with both sets of grandparents, but I have patients in my practice who have not, either because the grandparent has died, or the relationship between parent and grandparent is complicated and does not allow for such closeness to develop.

In these cases, just because someone didn't have a parent-like relationship with their grandparent, doesn't mean their loss isn't significant. Perhaps they love their grandparent dearly but never felt they had the opportunity to spend as much time with them as they would have liked. Some grandchildren lose their grandparent well before they are old enough to have a deep and mature relationship with them. When a grandparent dies, some people may be left with regret about unanswered questions and things left unsaid, as well as wishes about how they think the relationship 'could have' or 'should have' been. Professionals should pay attention to these reactions and use them as opportunities to have a conversation with the child, ask them if anything has changed at home, and give them the space and opportunity to tell you their grandparent has died. They may be reluctant to share this, but with some gentle questioning, this will open up a space for them to do so.

Often, family members consider the eldest family member to be the patriarch or matriarch of the family. This person may seem like the family's foundation, the person who is the 'glue' and holds the family together. When that person dies the entire family becomes fractured and untethered. Suddenly they are at a loss to know how to handle conversations because their mediator has gone. There are breakdowns in communication, no one knows who should host Thanksgiving or Christmas, and people start wondering if maybe they should skip the annual family reunion because it just won't be the same. In the vacuum of their loss, fear steps in and closes up their hearts. For some families they literally don't know how to start having direct conversations with one another because generally they have not had to learn how to do so. This is an opportunity to renew family ties, and one of the ways to start doing that is to talk about the person who has died – to thicken the family narrative – tell stories about that person, what you liked, didn't like, what made you laugh, cry, etc., so that this functions as a bridge between the old and the new phase.

If you are new to this kind of talk you can turn this into a game to help break the ice. Memories are all that we have left when a person has died so this helps to keep those memories alive. Gather your family together and sit in a circle. Invite each person to say something they liked about the person who has died. Don't worry if this gets off to a slow start, it will gather pace once people start to talk. When I do this activity with groups, it's not long before the stories start to link together. This comes from the stories jogging people's memories, and it's like a ball rolling downhill. Set a time limit on this game because it can be quite tiring if the bereavement is recent, maybe half an hour to start with. What one person forgets the other person remembers and this can be cathartic and healing for grieving families who find comfort in this narrative bonding.

'At least she lived a good long life'. This is something people love to say about grandparents, I guess because it's often true. It's not that helpful in grief, though, because being reminded of a person's age does nothing to ease the pain caused by their absence. There is never a point where you sit back and say – 'I think we've spent enough time together. Yes, I have plenty of memories in my grandpa memory bank, so I'm okay with losing you now'.

The person who has died is important and loved. So when someone minimizes their loss, even by saying it was expected, it can make it feel like they are undermining the person's significance and taking away their right to feel pain and sadness. Try saying something else like: 'Tell me about all the memories you have in your grandpa memory bank.'

People minimize losses for a handful of reasons. Some may assume loss isn't significant based on their belief that it is the expected, natural order for grandparents to die first. Some may make judgements based on their subjective experience that grandparents are distant, non-nuclear relatives, while some may realize how much pain children are in but offer the wrong words of comfort.

Just remember, children's grief is a reflection of their unique relationship with their grandparent and their individual ability to cope with this loss. Your job is to enable the grieving child to tell their story, in their words. What we want to do is to accept the child's feelings, and to give them permission to express these as being a natural part of their grieving process. The use of metaphor and symbolic play helps us to do this. Reading a story to a child about a character who is struggling to sleep helps the grieving child to identify with the character and the solution the character finds.

Story 2.9 The ant who couldn't sleep

Arthur was heartbroken when his Grandma died. No one explained to Arthur where his Grandma had gone and he missed her a lot. To make matters worse, he was also having trouble sleeping at night, and during the day he couldn't stay awake during his classes.

Arthur and his Grandma were very close. Every Wednesday after school Arthur went to his Grandma's house for tea. She always made her lemon cake specially for Arthur, which she set out on his favourite plates, ones they had chosen together at the market. After tea, they played cards at the dining room table – Snap – which they played loudly, competing with one another in a good-natured way. Each time his Grandma won a round she whooped with laughter and threw her hands in the air as she rocked in her rocking chair. Arthur loved hearing his Grandma's laugh.

Before she died, Arthur's Grandma had made a request of him, and now Arthur lay awake at night remembering her words: 'One day Arthur, when I'm not here, will you look after Grandma's cards?' she said.

At the time, Arthur hadn't paid much attention to this. After all, his Grandma was old but she had always been around, and he couldn't imagine a time when she wouldn't be making his cake and playing Snap with him.

After her funeral, Arthur went to his Grandma's house with his Mum to collect her cards. When he opened the door the first thing he noticed was his Grandma's empty chair. No cake lay on the plates. No tea in the pot. And no Grandma's laugh. Her found her cards in their pack beside her bed. Arthur sat on the bed and picked up the cards, feeling sad.

'Do you think Grandma knows how much I miss her?' asked Arthur. Do you think she is making her lemon cake for someone else now?' he asked.

'Yes, I think Grandma knows because I'm sure Grandma misses you very much,' said his Mum. 'And no, I think Grandma only made her lemon cake for you,' she said

Over the next few weeks Arthur became more and more restless at night and found it difficult to sleep through the night. He'd wake up thinking about his Grandma and then couldn't go back to sleep. He'd talk to his teddy as his Mum had told him to do, but when that didn't work and he was still wide awake, he'd get out of bed and wake his Mum up. She came into his room and read to him in bed until he fell asleep again, but in the morning, Arthur felt tired.

One night, as Arthur sat in bed trying to read his book, his feelers started to shake.

Arthur's Mum came into his room to kiss him goodnight.

'I have no one to play cards with now Grandma isn't here,' Arthur said.

'I know,' his Mum said.

'We all miss Grandma,' she said, 'but she lived a good, long life.'

Arthur felt sad, like someone had piled a heavy load of stones on top of his heart.

'But, I didn't get to tell Grandma EVERYTHING!' he cried.

His Mum leaned in to Arthur and gently said

'Neither did I,' she said.

She gently touched Arthur's face, wiped away his tears.

Arthur looked at his Mum, she had tears in her eyes again.

'You didn't?' he said.

'I wish I had told Grandma how much I loved her, just one more time,' she said.

Arthur breathed out heavily.

'Grandma was old, but when you love someone no amount of time together feels like enough,' she said quietly.

Arthur noticed how quiet his room was – no noises, he couldn't hear anything apart from his Mum's voice.

'So I'm wondering Arthur what you would like to have said to Grandma,' his Mum said.

Arthur felt the words bubbling up in his throat. He felt a bit scared and anxious so he quickly sat up in bed and blurted out:

'I wish I'd told her how much I loved her lemon cake, and how no one made my tea like she did,' he said.

Arthur's Mum stroked his hair. 'Would it help if you wrote Grandma a letter and told her about the other stuff?' she said.

Arthur's eyes widened.

'Yes, I could tell her that I will look after her cards,' he said 'I don't want Grandma to think I've forgotten the promise I made her,' he said.

'Well, I think that's a wonderful idea Arthur, and tomorrow we will buy some paper for you to write your letter to Grandma,' she said.

Arthur could feel his eye lids drooping.

'Maybe we could eat some cake afterwards, Mum,' Arthur said, yawning.

'Maybe we can,' she said smiling at him.

'Good night Arthur, sleep well,' his Mum said.

Arthur was already asleep dreaming of lemon cake.

What can I do to help?

Suggest the child writes a letter to the deceased in which they say everything they felt they did not say when they were alive. For children this can cover the small and big things.

Key messages

- **The denial message:** *Grandma lived a good long life* (isn't helpful if the child feels they have missed out on saying things to their grandparent).
- **The resilient message:** *Grandma was old – when you love someone no amount of time together feels like enough. What would you like to say to her in your letter?*

Classroom activity

Appetizer: Make a dreamcatcher

These are simple and can be made in 15 minutes. At the Craft Station in Outpatients, my team and I never knew how long we would have a child sitting at the crafting station for before the doctor called them in for their appointment. Sometimes the child sat crafting for just 15 minutes, but that was enough time to make a dreamcatcher. The key was having the 'ingredients' ready to make them. When the child returned to the hospital the following week for further tests or treatment, the parents would tell us how helpful the dreamcatcher had been for the child in terms of easing their anxiety. So, assemble the following items into a small, mobile, hand carrying container:

- Coloured card and tissue paper
- Glue
- Pipe cleaners
- Scissors
- Felt tip pens.

Explain to the child the purpose of the dreamcatcher, which is to catch bad dreams. Invite the child to draw a circle and cut this out. Invite them to decorate this. Ask them to choose some coloured paper and cut this into strips for them. This direct action not only saves time, but also helps the child to feel supported and nurtured. Finish off the dreamcatcher by sticking a pipe cleaner to the top so that this can either be pinned or stuck to the bedhead or, side table, wherever the child wants to keep it. Congratulate them on making this dreamcatcher and invite them to tell you about their experience of it. Keep this part light because they may not want to, but at least you have given them the opportunity to circle back to you.

Making dreamcatchers can be expanded into a small group or class activity where children learn about how their brains benefit from having this small container to hold their anxieties and worries.

Main course: Circle time

Gather your family together and sit in a circle. Invite each person to say something they liked about the person who has died. Don't worry if this gets off to a slow start, it will gather pace once people start to talk. When I do this activity with groups, it's not long before the stories start to link together. This comes from the stories jogging people's memories, and it's like a ball rolling downhill. Set a time limit on this game because it can be quite tiring if the bereavement is recent, maybe half an hour to start with. What one person forgets the other person remembers and this can be cathartic and healing for grieving families who find comfort in this narrative bonding.

How to construct a therapeutic story using the hero's journey framework

Here is a story called Tilly Tea Pot which I have deconstructed for you so that you can see the sequence of writing a therapeutic story using the hero's journey framework. If you have a child who is not responding to other interventions, you could try using this framework to write a simple story to use with her.

Identify the emotional problem or issue.

Client feels isolated from her classmates because she is the only mixed-race child at school.

Set a therapeutic objective – what would you like to change?

To enable the client to feel at ease and engaged, and to recognize that being different also means being unique.

Think of a strategy to achieve the change

The client meets people who object to her being treated differently. This advocacy on her behalf enables the child to feel included in the group and to use her voice to own her uniqueness and recognize theirs.

Base the story on a metaphorical conflict in terms that the child can relate to – a character, a place, a plot – grappling with the same emotional problem as the child. What similar stories or real life experiences could be used?

The client is the only T pot made in a pottery factory that is put to one side because it has a crinkly spout.

Start constructing the story by thinking out the ending in outline

When the T Pot hears the other pots standing up for her she realizes that she's not alone and this gives her confidence to notice their differences, and the things that make her and them unique. The result is that the client stops feeling isolated because she feels connected to the group of pots, and is clear about her role and contribution to the T set.

Write the start – set the scene

Tilly is a T pot. She has been made in a factory called Pots R Us that specializes in making T sets. The factory specifications are rigid and don't make allowances for any differences, all T pots have to look the same. But Tilly comes out of The Kiln with a crinkly spout instead of a straight one, and she therefore cannot be included in the T set because she is different from her fellow T pots. This has never happened at the factory before, and no one including The Kiln knows what to do. Seeing Tilly standing alone on a table puzzles the other pots. They don't know what to say to Tilly, and this leaves Tilly feeling isolated and lonely sitting on the table by herself. She wonders why she isn't included with the other pots.

Reach a metaphorical crisis

Tilly sits by herself on the table watching the pots being painted: some are given dots, others stripes, and she notices that she isn't being given either. She does notice that she is the only pot with a crinkly spout, and she wonders if that is why she has been excluded. This makes her feel sad. The sugar bowls and T. pots are rattling their lids, and she thinks they are poking fun at her, and this makes her doubly sad. Instead of joining in she sits very still. She wants to shout at them and tell them that she's just like them really, but they are making so much noise she's afraid they won't hear her.

When The Box marches in with his lid open carrying a big roll of cellotape in his arms Tilly's worst fears look like they will come true. Tilly knows that The Box is getting ready to pack all the pots up into a T set and send them off to a customer who has bought them! The sudden prospect of the pots leaving Tilly all by herself create a hush in the factory as the lids stop rattling. The cream jug and the sugar bowl notice that Tilly is alone. They all move out of their huddle and stand in a line facing Tilly. Tilly moves to the edge of her table and stares at them, a lone tear slides down her spout.

Construct the shift, the change of direction using parallel learning situations. Use a bridge section to avoid moving too quickly

Tilly catches the eye of Billy, the milk jug. Billy is slowly lifting his spout to wave at Tilly. Tilly wrinkles her crinkles in a slow smile. When Billy realizes that Tilly wants to be friends with the other pots, and she's not sitting alone because she doesn't like them, he moves to the edge of the table and speaks out in Tilly's defence. He challenges Mr Conveyer Belt and tells him that if Tilly isn't part of their T set and coming with them in the packing then they have no business calling the factory Pots R Us. Billy thought they were a team.

Billy is the leader of the pot gang, and when he speaks out in Tilly's defence all the other pots listen to him.

The Kiln hears the uproar and opens his door to find out what the noise is about. He's not used to being questioned about his power to mould and manufacture pots. He has a recipe to follow, a quota to fill, that's all he cares about. But Billy stands up to him and tells him that the pots are upset that Tilly won't be joining their T set. They are curious about Tilly's crinkles, and wonder why they don't have any.

Show the journey from crisis to positive solution and a new sense of identification

Tilly is surprised and delighted by Billy's advocacy, and the fact that the other pots really do want her to join their T set. This feeling of empathy encourages her to look more closely at herself and at her fellow pots. As she examines both she sees that not all their stripes and dots are the same as she had originally assumed. When she re-examines her own crinkles she realizes that she has more in common with her fellow pots than she thought. She notices the occasional dot in amongst her crinkles. This recognition of similarity makes her feel brave and excited about being at the beginning rather than the end of an adventure. Tilly suddenly moves closer to the edge of the table and finds the voice that she has been so nervous and scared of using. She claims her own identity as a crinkly T pot and announces that crinkles mean that she can pour in several directions and not just one! This announcement makes the other pots stand up proudly and say who they are – pots with wild stripes, lids with dazzling dots.

The Kiln is shocked by this show of collective team spirit, and for the first time marvels that the pots don't mind being different! What he thought were imperfections are actually marks of uniqueness. He apologizes to the pots and tells them that from now on he will change his control panel setting from 'different' to 'unique'.

End the story with a celebration and sense of community

The Kiln instructs The Box to carry Tilly from her lonely table to join the other pots. But Tilly stops him. She raises her crinkly spout and says that she wants to make that journey by herself. As she says this she takes a small step and joints the pots on their table. As she steps over the gap she notices that the gap between the two tables is tiny, and not as wide and cavernous as she had originally thought it was.

Tilly joins up the dots with the stripes and together they make a huge and colourful zigzag that dances around the shed. The Kiln turns on his lights and lights up the factory shed with warm light, and the whole T. set assembles on a blanket to enjoy their own special T. party.

Alternatively, the other story framework you could use in the classroom is the adapted 6PSM.

Chapter 3

Resolution

If we own the story then we can write the ending.

Brene Brown

Unresolved grief might seem an odd topic to include in a book aimed at helping children. You might wonder what this topic has to do with me helping children? In my experience of helping children cope with loss and change, one of the biggest challenges for caregivers is learning how not to be triggered by their children's behaviour. In a classroom there are around 30 opportunities for a teacher to be triggered each day, so I thought it would be helpful to include some general guidelines to help adults.

It's important to recognize our own issues so that we can stay fully present and empathic when children tell us their stories of loss and reveal their issues about meaning, identity, ambivalence, attachment and hope (Boss, 2006). In my experience of working with bereaved children and families, the learning goes both ways, or it can if we remain open to the lessons this path offers. In the midst of the heartbreak of loss and change is where we paradoxically find the opportunity to revisit, revise, refresh our own understanding about meaning, identity, ambivalence, attachment and hope. Obviously if the loss is 'fresh' particular care will need to be taken around finding meaning in this early stage. A good rule is be led by the family and test how open they are to you offering direct support to their child in school.

Finding an empathic response when we are grieving can be hard. Our grief can feel like an over-crowded room. We may feel so discomforted by its proximity that it's difficult to find space in which to explore someone else's grief. Grieving is a thing all by itself which can feel, at times, like a full-time job which fills up every area of our life. If we can maintain our capacity for resilience in the face of grieving by adapting, changing, growing and evolving, our core identity remains recognizable. But sometimes, the opposite happens – we end up parking this overwhelming loss – placing it either inside ourselves, burying it or, displacing it by throwing ourselves into external events or relationships or by being endlessly busy. Both are coping strategies to try and stave off the impact grief can have on us. Fundamentally, we don't want anything to change, to be different, so we resist, and this is where problems can arise. Either way, we may end up compartmentalizing our grief so that we are never transformed. I believe grief isn't something to 'get over', it is an experience that we have which has the capacity to change and transform us, if we allow it to. This requires our full cooperation, which means a general willingness to acknowledge the fact that change after loss is inevitable and to try and be open to whatever the changes bring. So what happens when we get stuck in our grief and lose our capacity for reflecting, changing, growing and evolving?

In this chapter I am exploring how we can feel empathic towards ourselves, especially in relation to the children we work with, in the context of unresolved grief. The mirror that we look into within ourselves may actually help us to reflect back to children who are struggling with their grief. Healing and transformation is possible if we apply a standard of self-care that enables us to learn when feel ready to move and shift alongside the changes and when we need to slow the process of change down.

Increasing our own comfort with ambiguity and loss

When my Mum died, I considered giving up my clinical practice. The prospect of being with bereaved children felt like an overwhelming ache when I was grieving hard myself. I did take time out in the immediate aftermath and used that time to recover my tenuous balance. As I stood at the precipice of my emotional loss and void, my wise clinical supervisor told me that far from being afraid of my loss, I should try and see it as helpful. I remember thinking, 'That feels impossible right now.' Remember, she said, we can only take our clients as far as we have gone ourselves. For example, it's more difficult to give someone directions if you haven't been there yourself or, even looked at the map! I sat with those words for a long time before realizing that if I closed my practice, it was highly likely that I would never open it again. I would be too fearful. I didn't want to stay fearful; my Mum would not have wanted that for me. She wanted me to reach new heights, always, and so I sat in the room with the children holding my grief and theirs. This was by far the most generative and transformative time in my clinical practice. The children definitely picked up my vulnerability which gave them permission to show me theirs. One child in particular, who had recently lost his Mum, was able to show me just how raw his feelings were through his play. The therapeutic relationship we built helped to heal us both. Being real doesn't mean having no boundaries. It's important to create strong yet flexible boundaries around children, enough so they feel you are accessible and not closed off. If you feel that you could benefit from learning more about boundaries I have included an exercise in the appendices. I understand that teachers are having their boundaries tested regularly and it's important to feel confident that they are strong as well as flexible. I didn't verbally share the details of my loss with this child; I held both the loss and the hope for renewal. This feels like the ocean ebbing and flowing, it's never stagnant. I didn't talk about my loss but the fact that I wasn't hiding it either gave the children permission to grieve more openly. Owning this loss has made me a better therapist.

The beginning of emotional support

At the risk of sounding like a self-help junkie, I have presented this chapter in a question-style format. This is an invitation for you to do some self-assessment and personal enquiry in areas that are touched when we lose someone or something we love. These areas of enquiry I have looked at myself in my quest for personal growth and transformation and they continue to offer me opportunities for self-reflection. The purpose of these activities for you is to allow you to do the same with the intention of developing and flexing your emotional muscles and resilience.

The problem of unresolved grief

When I'm looking at any concept or problem, I always look at the opposite of that problem because therein lies my solution. For example, letting go only works if you have something new to focus on. You can't just let go. Children who are clingy stop being so when they discover their safety position or person. What they never do is stop being clingy because we tell them to. Some people open a book and then turn straight to the back page to read the ending! I am one of those people. Working backwards has always helped me to know what steps I need to take to move forwards, to get the end result I want. And so it is with unresolved grief. Maybe one of the difficulties with resolving grief is that it feels overwhelming. Grief is grief, and I don't think it's something we fix or get over. The key is to work out what aspects we want to resolve.

For me, grief remains unresolved when our capacity to change becomes diminished, when we stop ourselves from being changed by the experience of loss. We can't accept the finality of the loss, so we resist the transition, the changes loss brings, and the rituals that mark out our life stop, cease to exist. For example, a baby dies and birthdays become impossibly difficult to recognize. Part of coping with loss and change involves holding ambivalence – as Carlos Sluzki says: do we welcome another year of life or, do we regret the passage of time? Do we celebrate our kid's first day of school or, mourn the loss of his or her family-centred, home-bound life? Do we express joy for a graduation or convey our sympathy for the beginning of a life of work? Do we throw rice and confetti with our blessings to the newlyweds or, do we shower them with pessimistic advice for a safe navigation of the unchartered and perhaps dangerous territory ahead? Social rules and mores give us normative ways of behaving and instructions about our feelings, they carry us through times of transition and change, but, when loss intrudes on these rules and changes them, that is when our capacity for change is truly tested.

When we are struggling with unresolved grief, the risk is that our capacity for coping with situations that touch that grief may be reduced. So, a grieving child may trigger that inner child we all carry with us who may also be grieving.

In his anthology *Reclaiming the Inner Child*, editor Jeremiah Abrams says that the

> 'inner child is the carrier of our personal stories, the vehicle for our memories of both the actual child and an idealized child from the past. It is the truly alive quality of being within us. It is the soul, our experiencer throughout the cycles of life. It is the sufferer. And it is the bearer of renewal through rebirth, appearing in our lives whenever we detach and open to change'. (Jeremiah Abrams, 1990, *Reclaiming the Inner Child*, Los Angeles: Jeremy P. Tarcher)

If you are struggling to hear and give your inner child space, there are many exercises you can do, and I refer you to work of Cathryn L. Taylor and her book *The Inner Child Workbook: What to do with Your Past when it Just Won't Go Away*. This is deep inner healing work and probably best done with the support of a therapist.

If we are struggling with this ourselves, we will also struggle to help a child through this stage, so I always recommend investing in looking at this area with creative and therapeutic tools. I recommend completing the 'object relations' exercise which will enable you to access more of your inner child's voice.

Case study

A father of one of my clients, Brian, lost his wife in her early 30s. They had only been married five years and had a young child. His wife died of cancer and Brian nursed her throughout her illness. As a self-employed man with his own business, he struggled to take the time out from his work to care for his wife, especially when she reached the palliative care stage. His young son had just started primary school and was struggling with the changes his Mother's illness and subsequent death brought. Following his wife's death, Brian began a relationship with a woman almost immediately, and after six months they married. Brian's coping strategy was to say that the 'past is the past and I've moved on'. The problem was that in an attempt to skip over his grief, Brian tapped right into his pain. This manifested itself in angry rages at his young son who desperately needed his Father's attention, but Brian could not allow himself to nurture his son because he reminded him of his dead wife. It was a very sad and tragic situation for the family, and my hope was that at some point, Brian would be able to allow himself to feel his grief and to accept his loss, but he didn't. Brian saw his son's deteriorating behaviour as 'naughtiness' rather than the acting out of his own grief, and could not feel any empathy towards his son. Was this really surprising given that Brian could not feel any connection to his own feelings?

What Brian couldn't do was accept the changes caused by the loss of his wife and this made it hard for him to see the impact of those changes in the way his son was behaving.

I realized during this case that when we don't allow ourselves to feel the pain of our losses, we also can't make any connection to ourselves or, to anyone else. Finding meaning becomes more difficult. We feel insecure, uncertain about our present and future and finding peace becomes illusive. As Brene Brown (TED talk) says, we can't selectively numb our emotions, for when we numb the painful emotions, we also numb the positive emotions, like joy, gratitude and happiness. When we engage in numbing behaviour we also dissociate ourselves. One drawback of the disease model of addiction is that it fails to address the millions of people who try and escape their feelings in ways that are troublesome and perhaps take their toll, but diagnostically don't qualify as addiction. Like watching Netflix, talking on the phone with friends. Obviously it's about finding a place on the spectrum where we can self-soothe but not to the extent that we are in denial of our feelings. And our feelings are right at the centre of our losses.

So, how do we learn to navigate towards accepting the changes caused by loss?

I propose that perhaps the way to soften unresolved grief is to look at the areas of our lives that are often affected by loss and change, some of which may feel torn, in an attempt to rebuild ourselves after loss.

So, what areas do we need to look at and soften?

- **Courage** to bear the unbearable and embrace uncertainty.
- **Comfort** with boundaries and language.
- **Creativity** to find meaning and change the narrative.

Courage to bear the unbearable and embrace uncertainty

Sometimes grief just needs to be expressed directly and simply, but this is often the most unbearable aspect of our grief. Saying so makes it real and present because it's finally coming face to face with uncertainty, the fact that we don't have control over every aspect of our lives.

When Joanne Cacciatore's young daughter died, she struggled to find anyone who could really listen to her grief. She saw three therapists and they all, in different ways, could not hold her pain. One suggested she go to church, the second referred her to a psychiatrist for medication and the third just 'didn't get it'. When she broke down in her home, her 3-year-old daughter heard her crying and said, 'Oh Mummy, it's okay to cry and it's okay to be sad because babies aren't supposed to die.' She felt tremendous gratitude for the wisdom and compassion of this little girl who helped her to bear the unbearable.

I believe grief creeps into our consciousness even when we are desperately trying to shut it out. It will force its way through into situations whether we like it or not – causing us to break down at a party in front of friends or strangers, shout at someone in the grocery store because they don't have our favourite fruit and yell at random drivers on the roads. These can be symptoms of us trying to ignore our feelings so for me, the question really becomes: what circumstance do I need to create in order to be heard? Who or what will help me to bear the unbearable?

Therapeutic writing can be helpful in getting clear about what you need to create to be heard, and the act itself will enable you to tap directly into the feelings you are finding unbearable. If you set a timer for this exercise, say 30 minutes, you safeguard becoming overwhelmed. I recommend going back to the writing the following day after a night's sleep. You will be surprised how much insight you have captured onto the page! This is one of my trainee's most favoured exercises. It's a good idea to complement this writing exercise with the 15-minute 'drawing check-in' exercise which I recommend you do first.

Comfort with boundaries and language

Boundaries can be a big issue when dealing with grief generally. People often mean well but, unless they are giving us something we want, the help can feel inappropriate, intrusive and unwanted. This can range from the people who try to cheer you up with a funny story, to people who share their own grief story in the hope that you might find some relief. Grief can make people feel awkward and these are usually clumsy attempts to say something! One of the grieving children in my practice found a creative solution for this problem. He made himself a small cardboard sign that he hung around his neck. On one side he wrote the words 'Please talk to me' and on the other side he wrote 'Please give me space today'. The sign helped him set his boundaries after his Father died and he couldn't keep repeating these messages to people. It was a genuine way for him to feel safe around others. This sign really helped his peers and teachers to know when it was ok to approach him and stopped them from feeling embarrassed. A simple and brilliant idea.

Creativity to find meaning and change the narrative

Every family has its own grief narrative, which originates around the way grief has been handled generationally. Older generations generally don't talk about grief and, if this has been the way grief has been handled in your family, chances are you will have picked up the message that grief is something you don't talk about. I was in my 40s before I developed a different grief narrative from my family's style which was to keep grief private, have a stiff sherry and go for a bracing walk! When I was diagnosed with ovarian cancer in 2002, I discovered that keeping my grief quiet was the last thing I wanted to do! I eventually went on national television to talk about raising awareness of ovarian cancer because I didn't want other young women to suffer as I had. This was my way of expressing my voice which came from a deep need of being heard. I'm not suggesting the route of activism is for everyone, but it was one way, just as writing is, that allowed me to express my voice.

Which leads me to creativity. Finding meaning after a loss can be difficult. Disorientated by the changes loss brings makes it tough to see the landscape going forward. '*What's left?*' '*What do I want?*' are some of the questions we ask ourselves. If the grief has been put to one side, for whatever reason, picking it up again can be made a little easier through a creative medium. I chose the medium of painting and art therapy to express my feelings of loss which appealed specifically because they were largely non-talking mediums. You have probably heard the expression 'I lost myself in that activity'; well, I did the opposite, I found myself again, and that woman could never have said out loud the things I discovered in the paint. I didn't want to die and I was afraid that I might, so rather than say those things out loud to my loved ones, who would have found them unbearable to hear, I expressed my feelings through colour and texture, and ended up painting over 200 paintings, right through my treatment and recovery. The medium helped me to save my life, no doubt, and eventually found its way into my first book *Coming to my Senses: Finding My Voice through Ovarian Cancer.* So if you are feeling stuck, blocked, cut off, shut down, unhinged even, ask yourself this: if today was my last day of breath, how would I express my last words? And go from there. You might discover that music is your thing and that banging the drums each week is your kind of outlet. Whatever your chosen outlet is, use this as if it were your last hope, because it might end up saving you.

Toolkit

Just as I have created resources for children, so I have created resources for adults in the form of a story. The intention in using this story is to enable adults to experience the feelings that arise after reading a story about loss. I have used this particular story during my workshops with counsellors and grief workers and they have found it helpful on two levels. One level is giving themselves the time and space to look at their own feelings and reactions, which can feel like a luxury in itself, to step back and away from the sharp end of holding someone else's grief, and the second level is suddenly developing a new empathy for the way in which children might experience loss. The act of being read to and listening to a story transports people into their feelings quickly. The point about doing this exercise is really about creating a connection with yourself. Once we feel that strong connection it is easier to develop empathy because we have a pot to draw from. If you are running on emotional empty or burn out, which I discuss in Chapter 4, it is much harder to have an empathic response.

How to use this story

You will need to gather a few creative resources: coloured pens and pencils and two sheets of A4 paper. One sheet is to draw on, the second sheet is for you to write down your feelings. Set these out on a table within easy reach.

Before I read this story out loud to a group of people, I set out some ground rules. These equally apply to you reading this story by yourself. It's all about preparing your mind and body to be as receptive as possible, and we do that by putting aside technology and sitting comfortably. So:

- Turn off your cell phone.
- Put down your paper and pens.
- Turn off your computer/laptop/tablet.
- Find a quiet space to sit where you will not be disturbed for one hour.
- Uncross your legs or ankles.
- Sit up straight in your chair.
- Keep your eyes open.

Eric and the frog

Eric lived with his Mum and Dad near the woods. Every day before and after school Eric ran outside and played in the woods. Every day he found new treasure, a stone to add to his collection, a feather to build a nest with. There was a never ending supply of rocks and wood that Eric could make things out of. One morning Eric found something very different in the woods … something he had never seen before. Eric's eyebrows shot up and his heart started racing. It was a bullfrog! Very green and very large lying on his side making a sound that reminded Eric of his sister choking on her food.

Eric ran over to the frog thinking it might be dead but he saw that the frog's eyes were slowly blinking and he realized he was still alive. Eric wondered what to do – he didn't want to be late for school but he couldn't just leave this poor frog fighting to breathe so, he ran back to his house to call his Mum.

'Mum, come quick, I've found a frog in the woods and I think he needs help. Bring water!' Eric shouted. He filled a small plant pot with water from the garden hose and walked as quickly as he could back to the woods. He hoped the frog was still alive, he hoped he wasn't too late.

Meanwhile his Mum, looking out the window, saw Eric filling the pot with water and called his Dad. His Dad called his sister, who brought a wet towel and, pretty soon they were all gathered together in the woods looking at the frog with Eric.

Eric knelt down next to the frog and quietly dabbed him with water from his pot. The frog's choking sounds eased off and he stopped blinking his eyes. Eric looked at his Dad. 'Don't frogs live in ponds?' he said. His Dad nodded. 'Hold on, frog' said Eric. 'We are going to find you a pond and you will be home soon.' The frog let out a little sigh.

Then everyone worked together to find the pond in the woods. Eric's sister found it first: 'It's over here!' she shouted. Eric and his Mum carefully lifted the frog onto a wet towel and carried him to the pond. Eric was holding his breath, willing the frog to stay alive. They released the frog into the water and saw the life come back into him. His legs quivered and he wriggled his body as he began to swim in the water.

Eric stood up and let out a loud cheer: 'Yay, we did it!'

The next day, Eric returned to the pond to check on his frog. He looked at all sides of the pond and eventually sat down and stared at the water watching it for any ripples. Finally his Mum came to find him, and put her arm around him. She said, 'I am really proud of you, Eric.' Then they slowly walked back to the house together.

Take several deep breath inhalations through your nose, until you can feel your rib cage expanding, then breathe out through your mouth.

Now you are ready to read the story. Read the story through once, either out loud or, to yourself, whichever you prefer; either way is fine.

Now you have finished reading the story, put the piece of paper down beside you and close your eyes. Sit quietly for a few minutes in your chair. Let whatever feelings you have arise. Notice them and give them a name. Open your eyes and select some coloured pens and pencils, whichever colour you feel drawn to, and take the first sheet of paper you have set aside. On this, draw a representation of your feelings. Spend 5 minutes creating your drawing with as much detail as you like. Try not to critique yourself while drawing! This is not about creating perfection, it's only about getting down on paper an image that captures the feeling. This image can be whatever you want it to be! You are free to make this picture as big or small as you like. The only rule is, the drawing must be on one side of A4.

When you have completed the drawing put this down on the table and spend a few quiet minutes looking at this. When you are ready, pick up the second sheet of blank A4 paper and write down the answers to these questions:

- How do you feel about the drawing itself?
- What do you notice about the drawing?
- What do you like and dislike about the drawing?
- What surprises you about the colours you have chosen?
- In what way would you like to change this drawing?

You will remember from reading the children's stories, that this exercise is about creating a dialogue between three areas: your mind (racing thoughts), body (sweating, breathing difficulties) and feelings (sad, anger).

So now let's circle back to where we started this conversation, and ask ourselves how we are feeling about unresolved grief. Are you clearer about what needs resolving?

Resilience

Resilient people look at a problem and say, what's the solution, what is this trying to teach me.

Anon

Words often associated with the concept of resilience are, 'bouncing back', 'toughness', or 'struggle'. I remember hearing the actress Annette Bening being interviewed about her ability to bounce back after giving birth to her children. 'I don't bounce back,' she replied. 'I take my time to recover.' Wise words. In my experience it is rare that anyone bounces back after tragedy, loss and heartache. Instead, what builds resilience is learning the lesson and making changes in our communication style and attitude towards self-care.

We are changed inside and out by loss and can choose whether or not to accept the lesson and wisdom from the change. This takes time, energy, commitment, guts and grit certainly to adjust to and cope with. Where I am tough and where I believe toughness is called for is in doing the work necessary to cope with loss and change and to create resilience through making those changes. That process requires commitment and dedication.

The American Psychological Association defines resilience thus: 'Resilience is that ineffable quality that allows some people to be knocked down by life and come back stronger than ever. Rather than letting failure overcome them and drain their resolve, they find a way to rise from the ashes.' Psychologists have identified some of the factors that make someone resilient, among them a positive attitude, optimism, the ability to regulate emotions, and the ability to see failure as a form of helpful feedback. Even after misfortune, resilient people are blessed with such an outlook that they are able to change course and soldier on.

I would add to this my process called 'unpacking your emotional backpack' which helps us to see the lesson.

Case study

The G family came to see me because their daughter (8 years of age), was having angry meltdowns. The Father, a hospital consultant, was by his own admission engaged in a power struggle with his daughter and feeling at the end of his tether. The Mother, a primary care nurse, was also struggling to control her temper, especially when her daughter would not follow her instructions. This often resulted in angry shouting matches between the parents and their daughter. Resilience levels were very low for them all. During the consultation assessment with the parents I could feel how hot the emotional temperature was inside this family. I agreed to see the daughter for 12 sessions of play therapy and during that time, the parents also got on board and began to unpack their own heavy backpacks. I don't think they had realized how destructive the exchanges had grown between them all. The most amazing breakthrough in this family, which you can listen to live on my website, is how the parents' resilience levels increased when they realized that they weren't actually listening to their daughter's concerns and feelings. The difficulty with this was due to the fact that the parents disagreed with their daughter's concerns and dismissed them as unimportant. This dismissal angered their daughter and was at the root of all their arguments. Once they understood that they didn't have to agree all the time with their daughter's concerns, but they did have to acknowledge her feelings as valid, they were able to step back from the confrontation and ask her what she was concerned about, instead of railroading her by telling her that her concerns weren't important. This shifted the whole family dynamic so much that meltdowns are a rare occurrence now. The family has developed my backpack metaphor even further by creating a family picnic where each person unpacks their backpack! This helps them all to unload their worries. As professionals we also carry backpacks and it is important to know how this can affect us and what we can do about it.

Overcoming compassion fatigue and laying the foundation for wellness

Over time, professionals working in loss and bereavement can burn out and suffer what Eric Gentry calls 'compassion fatigue', the result of witnessing trauma, otherwise known as 'the cost of caring' (Figley, 1995).

The level of compassion fatigue a person experiences can change from one day to the next, and even very healthy people with optimal life/work balance and self-care strategies can experience a higher-than-normal level of compassion fatigue when they are overloaded and are working with a lot of traumatic content. This is especially relevant for teaching professionals who have bereaved children in their class, and whose family circumstances have been dramatically affected by their loss. In these circumstances, teaching professionals may be expressing higher than usual levels of compassion and empathy which over time can lead to compassion fatigue, especially if those professionals don't have anyone or anywhere to express their feelings associated with supporting bereaved children. Compassion fatigue can have a sudden onset, but it is treatable, whereas burnout usually emerges over time. The other potential complication is adult unresolved grief which, if untreated, can contribute to burnout.

Symptoms of compassion fatigue

Compassion fatigue can take a physical, mental, spiritual and emotional toll on people who experience it. Common symptoms of compassion fatigue include:

- Chronic physical and emotional exhaustion
- Depersonalization

- Feelings of inequity towards the therapeutic or caregiver relationship
- Irritability
- Feelings of self-contempt
- Difficulty sleeping
- Weight loss
- Headaches
- Poor job satisfaction.

How can compassion fatigue be prevented?

Practising self-awareness and self-monitoring to recognize changes in behaviour, work and life outside work is the first step to preventing compassion fatigue. Developing either informal or formal supervisory and mentor relationships within your work environment can also help you spot when you are being affected by compassion fatigue.

These three steps can also help build professional resilience and prevent compassion fatigue:

- *Learning the lesson* – (unpacking your emotional backpack and meeting your true, authentic self in the creative mediums)
- *Communicating compassionately* – (improving the quality of communication skills and relationships necessary to optimize professional relationships and the ability to work in teams, while improving their efficiency and enjoyment of working practically with children)
- *Evaluating self-care* – (self-awareness, mindfulness, finding meaning in the stories we hear, counter-transference, and physical exercise) by identifying triggers.

Often, people experiencing compassion fatigue will seek the professional support of a mental health clinician to help them overcome difficult thoughts and emotions and focus on healthy coping mechanisms.

Step 1: Learning the lesson through unpacking your emotional backpack

Teaching professionals who experience compassion fatigue usually do so because they struggle to prioritize their own emotional needs. The empathy and compassion they give to the children in the classroom can drain them if they are not regularly unpacking their emotional backpack. Like the children, they can get overloaded with their worries, anxieties and stresses. When your backpack is overflowing, the children will most likely trigger an emotional response in you which has nothing to do with the children.

Unpacking your emotional backpack enables you to have difficult conversations without being triggered, and enjoy a happier, more connected relationship with the children in your classroom. Additionally, you will feel lighter in mind and heart, have more energy, be more accessible to the children, not lose your temper as often and make clearer decisions.

Whatever lesson you need to learn will be buried somewhere inside your backpack. Taking things out slowly will help you to find this. If it helps, compare this sorting out process to sorting out your laundry basket! Some preparation is involved. Instead of loading all your laundry into the washing machine in one go, you might choose to sort this into piles first, according to colour, textile and washing instructions. Then you do each load individually. So it is with unpacking your backpack. You will be unpacking three piles:

Pile 1: Crisis – take off your mask to get clarification

This is where you will learn to differentiate between your ego, core self, projected self and true authentic self. You are going to do a mask exercise here, and discover things such as where you are being the victim, tune into your stress signals, and learn how your body communicates to you when it is feeling overwhelmed (for example, do you get sick as soon as you go on vacation or, get a migraine when you are stressed?) This will help you to sharpen your intuition and make connections between what you need and what you can get rid of. Completing this exercise can be powerfully liberating as you begin to see just how much you have been carrying around that no longer serves you.

Pile 2: Connection – write your core story

This will help you to find your voice, and understand more about who you truly are, underneath all the negative chit chat that we all have going on inside our heads. Writing a story can help to unlock psychophysical suffering by showing us what we have internalized, i.e. generational scripts that don't belong to us but which we have inherited from our parents. Carrying these around and listening to them can affect our entire outlook and decision making process, so becoming more self-aware helps us to understand why our buttons can get pressed. This helps you to find the right level of empathic engagement because you start to understand where your boundaries are.

Pile 3: Centre – story board who you are now

This is the more playful part! In this section you bring all your learning together and create a visual story board of who you are now as well as what you need and want in your life. It's an opportunity to visualize things as you want them to be versus how they have been.

Step 2: Communicating compassionately with colleagues, parents and multi-agencies

This section is based on Marshall Rosenberg's four-part Compassionate Communication Model, also known as Nonviolent Communication (NVC), using the term 'nonviolence' as Gandhi used it to refer to our natural state of compassion when violence has subsided from the heart. While we may not consider the way we talk to be 'violent', words often lead to hurt and pain, whether for others or ourselves. This is especially true in the field of loss and bereavement where we encounter children whose feelings are raw, which in turn might arouse similar feelings in adults. NVC replaces our old patterns of defending, withdrawing, or attacking in the face of judgement and criticism, so we begin to perceive ourselves and others in a compassionate way.

Nonviolent Communication includes a simple method for clear, empathic communication consisting of four areas of focus:

- Observations
- Feelings
- Needs
- Requests.

NVC aims to find a way for all present to get what really matters to them without the use of guilt, humiliation, shame, blame, coercion or threats. It is useful for resolving conflicts, connecting with others, and living in a way that is conscious, present and attuned to the genuine, living needs of yourself and others.

Using the four-part process will enable professionals to reduce their stress and anxiety when communicating in this difficult context, which in turn will make it easier for them to hear and deal with the children's and parents' stress and anxiety and to:

- Build a partnership where the goal is compassionate communication.
- Lead and engage without blame or judgement.
- Be creative to encourage constructive parent involvement.
- Put the child first when dealing with different parental types.

There are three primary modes of application of NVC:

- **Self-empathy** involves compassionately connecting with what is going on inside us. This may involve, without blame, noticing the thoughts and judgements we are having, noticing our feelings, and most critically, connecting to the needs that are affecting us.

     Receiving empathically, in NVC, involves

     connection with what's alive in the other person and what would make life wonderful for them … It's not an understanding of the head where we just mentally understand what another person says … Empathic connection is an understanding of the heart in which we see the beauty in the other person, the divine energy in the other person, the life that's alive in them … It doesn't mean we have to feel the same feelings as the other person. That's sympathy, when we feel sad that another person is upset. It doesn't mean we have the same feelings; it means we are with the other person … If you're mentally trying to understand the other person, you're not present with them.

- Empathy involves 'emptying the mind and listening with our whole being'. NVC suggests that however the other person expresses themselves, we focus on listening for the underlying observations, feelings, needs and requests. It is suggested that it can be useful to reflect a paraphrase of what another person has said, highlighting the NVC components implicit in their message, such as the feelings and needs you guess they may be expressing.

- **Expressing honestly**, in NVC, is likely to involve expressing an observation, feeling, need and request. An observation may be omitted if the context of the conversation is clear. A feeling might be omitted if there is sufficient connection already, or the context is one where naming a feeling isn't likely to contribute to connection. It is said that naming a need in addition to a feeling makes it less likely that people will think you are making them responsible for your feeling. Similarly, it is said that making a request in addition to naming a need makes it less likely that people will infer a vague demand that they address your need. The components are thought to work together synergistically. According to NVC trainer Bob Wentworth an observation sets the context, feelings support connection and getting out of our heads, needs support connection and identify what is important, and a request clarifies what sort of response you might enjoy. Using these components together minimizes the chances of people getting lost in potentially disconnecting speculation about what you want from them and why.

Sentence templates

Sometimes, a memorized sentence template can help structure what you need to say:

- 'Are you feeling ____ because you need ____?' Empathize as well as you can to fill in the blanks, and you'll likely find yourself seeing the situation as the other person does.
- 'Are you angry because you're thinking ____?' Anger is triggered by thoughts like 'I think you lied' or 'I think I deserve a raise more than so-and-so did.' Uncover the thought, and you are on your way to uncovering the underlying need.
- 'I'm wondering if you're feeling ____' is another way to empathize, without explicitly asking a question. The phrasing makes clear that this is your guess, and not an attempt to analyse the other person or *tell* them what they are feeling. So moderate *your* statement of feelings or needs with simple words like 'if you might, how about, could this be, maybe …'.
- 'I see ____' or 'I'm hearing that ____' are ways to state an observation clearly so that the other person hears it as an observation.
- 'I'm thinking ____' is a way to express a thought so it is heard as a thought, which is capable of changing as you get new information or ideas.
- 'Would you be willing to ____?' is a clear way to make a request.
- 'Would you like it if I ____?' is a way to offer to help fulfil a need just identified, while leaving the other person still responsible for their own need.
- A complete template for all four steps could go: 'I see ____. I'm feeling ____ because I need ____. Would you be willing to ____?' Or, 'I see ____. Are you feeling ____ because you need ____?' followed by 'Would it help if I ____?' or a statement of your own feeling and need followed by a request.

Tips

- Avoid saying 'You made me feel ____', 'I feel ____ because you did ____,' and especially, 'You're making me angry.' These put responsibility for your feelings on the other person, and they skip identifying the need that is the true cause of your feeling. An alternative: 'When you did ____, I felt ____ because I needed ____.' On the other hand, as noted earlier, if less-explicit phrasing is communicating your needs just fine, without making one person responsible for another person's feelings, then it's not necessary to spell things out so fully.
- You can use the same four steps yourself to get clarity about your own needs and choose action intelligently. For example, if you're in a situation where you're upset, one approach is to berate yourself or others: 'These people are idiots! Don't they know they're ruining this whole project with their narrow-mindedness?' Nonviolent self-talk might go something like this: 'The other engineers were not convinced. I don't think they heard my case. I'm feeling upset because I'm not getting listened to the way I need. I want the respect that comes with getting the reasons for my design heard, and my design accepted. Now how can I get that respect? Maybe not from this team. Or maybe I could meet with some of the engineers one-on-one, when conversation is not so heated, and see where things go from there.'

Creating an ethical and sustainable self-care plan

The professional self-care plan is based around two of Gentry's principles:

- Development and maintenance of intentionality, through a non-anxious presence, in both personal and professional spheres of life.
- Development and maintenance of self-validation, especially self-validated care-giving.

A non-anxious presence refers to the ability of being in the room with the child's pain and suffering and being able to express empathy and compassion without taking on the other person's suffering. In both the personal and the professional realm, it is about mindfulness, the ability to notice and control your physical symptoms of stress and anxiety, and breathing.

'Self-validated caregiving' refers to self-care that is guilt-free, self-care that is prioritized as a means of remaining healthy in this line of work.

Developing a non-anxious presence

The simplest way to explain this concept of intentionality is to imagine that when you are facing the children in your classroom there is a silver lining between you and them. This silver lining is a piece of smooth, silky fabric which extends from you to them and functions as an invisible space between you. This fabric can be any shape you like. It might be a square or a circle. You can expand and contract this silver lining space as much as you like, depending on your comfort or anxiety level at the time of any interaction. This silver lining protects you from becoming too involved in or enveloped by the classroom tension and stress, conflicts and interactions.

Over time and with practice, you will come to visualize this silver lining easily in your mind. You are going to use creative visualization to create your silver lining. This exercise is to follow.

Self-validated care-giving plan

This contains exercises and resources in five key areas.

1. Self-awareness

Being in tune with your stress signals. Do you have a good sense of how your body communicates to you when it is overwhelmed? Do you get sick as soon as you go on vacation, develop hives, get a migraine when you are stressed?

Body stress mapping exercise
The best way to attune to your body's stress signals is to lie down! This exercise is designed to help you identify the areas in your body where you are holding your stress, which results in muscle tension. It's easier to tune into your body in a prone position rather than a sitting position. I recommend you do this exercise alone or, in pairs. In pairs you can swop notes at the end of the exercise, which can be useful in terms of gaining insights. If you are doing the exercise alone, write down your notes in your notebook and reflect on these afterwards with a coffee. Allow up to 1 hour to complete this

exercise. Choose a quiet space where you will not be disturbed and turn your phone to silent.

Materials you will need:

- A single roll of plain white decorating paper
- Coloured markers
- Scissors
- Four objects to keep the paper in place on the floor.

What you are going to do

Roll out the decorating paper on the floor until you have enough to lie down on. If you are 5 x 10, roll out 6 feet. Cut this paper and place your four objects, one at each corner of the paper, to secure the paper to the floor.

Choose one coloured marker. Lie down flat on top of the paper. Trace the outline around your body from head to toe.

Sit up and move off the paper leaving the paper secured to the floor. You should have a drawn outline of your body on the paper.

Now you are going to map out the areas of your body where you feel stressed, tired, tense, irritable, even angry. With the coloured markers, 'decorate' your body outline with your stress markers. For example, you might feel a tightness in your chest or throat, so some of the ways you can express this are to:

- Write down single words: I feel tight in my throat.
- Write down phrases: I feel a tightness in my chest when the children are noisy.
- Draw a picture on your throat, maybe in red marker, showing this tightness, maybe jagged or squiggly lines.

Do this for every area of your body where you feel that you are carrying stress. Don't be alarmed if you locate this in surprising areas! I have had professionals draw pictures on their toes and ears! The amazing thing about doing this exercise in this way is that it will start a dialogue between you and your body, which is something we can ignore when we are busy and convince ourselves that we don't have time to pay attention to. However, if we don't attend to these body signals, what tends to happen is that our body will do what I call, 'up the ante', it raises the bar in order to get our attention. For example, a muzzy head may turn into a blinding headache or migraine if we don't stop and deal with whatever is causing this muzzy head. By stopping I don't necessarily mean downing tools! I understand that this isn't always possible during a busy school day. So stopping can be giving yourself, 'a moment' where you acknowledge the tension to yourself and say to yourself that you will deal with this. For example, if you are feeling this muzzy head and a child or a colleague asks you to do something which you think might just tip you over the edge, take a moment and say, 'Can I think about that and get back to you in 15 minutes?' This buys you some time to, if necessary, go to the loo, close your eyes for two minutes, and attend to whatever is buzzing around in your head. Make a note of it so that you can circle back to this at the end of your day, when you will do your relaxation exercise to wind down.

When your body map is complete, make a note in your notebook of the areas that you want to pay attention to. For example, if your legs feel tight, you might decide to note down: schedule a walk outside in the countryside this weekend. Note that I didn't say, 'go to the gym'! While I'm not against going to the gym, I have noticed that this can be another thing to schedule and then give ourselves a hard time about when we don't make it to the gym.

So, whatever action you decide to take to counteract your body tension, make sure these are simple and easy actions to take. This will make it more likely that you will do them. I am a big fan of yoga and have a home practice. I noticed that when I gave myself the instruction to do this every day, I felt guilty when I missed a day. This feeling could stay with me and counteract any good feeling I might have had from actually doing the yoga so, instead, I focused on reminding myself how good I felt after doing my practice, how my body felt ready for the day because it had been warmed up and stretched after being asleep all night which put me in a better mindset to do my yoga practice. In this mindset I noticed I stepped onto my mat when I listened to my body rather than the head set chatter that berated me.

I recommend doing this exercise at the start of each new season because our bodies feel and react differently to heat and cold, so it's highly likely that whatever tension we are carrying will show up in different places. Think of this as your body MOT. After you've done this a few times you might notice that you aren't as susceptible to signing up for new exercise classes as you were before. This is because you are developing a body wisdom, which means that your body will tell you when it needs to stretch, run, walk, rest, etc., and all you have to do is listen to this wisdom and act on it.

The second part of this exercise is listening to a relaxation recording. This will help you to start honing your creative visualization skills. These skills will not only be useful to your personally but you may also be able to use them in the classroom too.

If you have time, you can listen to the relaxation recording before doing the body mapping exercise. This will enable you to go even deeper with developing your body wisdom.

2. Mindfulness

Learning how to stop emotionally numbing through being able to be fully present in the moment, and cope more ethically with the trauma arising.

Mindfulness is a now a huge topic with lots of material available online. If you want to learn about specific mindful techniques, please refer to these resources.

I teach a simple technique to be fully present which I have found useful in my clinical practice, and I call this 'the ONE click method'.

This was originally taught to me by my meditation teacher, Lee Everett, many years ago, and it is the quickest tool to being present to oneself and others. Over the years it has enabled me to bring my busy mind back to my present situation. What can happen in stressful situations is the mind goes into 'fight or flight' which means that we lose our connection to our rational thinking as our body adrenalin rises to an unhealthy level and we can overreact to a situation. This overreaction is something that we would not usually do, but at the time of reaction we can't see this, all we can feel is fear, so we 'take off' and can sound unreasonable and not ourselves. You will recognize this moment before 'take off' because your body might feel hot or flushed. What we want is to be able to stop ourselves from reaching this 'take off' point, and we can do that by using the ONE click method.

The ONE click method

If you know that you are going to be entering a potentially difficult situation that might make your blood pressure rise (!), I want you to, 'take 5 minutes' before entering that situation to use the ONE click method.

Find a quiet spot to take your 5 minutes. Loos are everywhere and I usually find this is the quietest place where I can be alone with my thoughts. No one will argue with you saying you need to use the loo! Go into the cubicle and close the door. Sit down on the closed seat. You will find that the doors of the loo function to shut out all the noise that might be trying to overwhelm your brain. Close your eyes and take a few moments to slow your breathing down. Breathe in through your nose and out through your mouth five times. You should start to feel calmer just from doing this. Open your eyes. Think about leaving the loo and entering the meeting calmly, and at this point raise your pen writing hand until it's at eye level and CLICK your fingers once, firmly. You should be able to hear the click clearly. In that CLICK feel yourself being fully present in your body. Stand up and stretch your arms up. Feel the tension leaving your body and being replaced with strength and energy. You are ready to leave the loo and enter your situation feeling calm and present.

Repeat this exercise as often as you like. You will eventually reach the stage where you don't have to use the loo to use the ONE click method because you will be able to simply visualize yourself doing this which will instantly bring you back into your body and present situation.

3. Containment

Making sense of the stories we hear – finding the right level of empathic engagement, starting with the self.

Teachers are containing children, stories and themselves all day, five days a week, which can be exhausting. Sometimes if we don't contain ourselves enough we can get a sense of losing ourselves, which just means we may start to feel disconnected from ourselves. This is when situations can feel distorted. We might misconstrue or misunderstand something a child or parent says to us, we might overreact, start taking things personally, etc. I have found that one way to help reconnect you to your true self and find a comfortable sense of containment again is through painting and creating a series of what I call Quest paintings. Again, this is an exercise I use in all my trainings and in my own self-care practice and which can be completed in one hour. Once you are familiar with the set-up and process of this exercise you can shorten it according to the time you have available. I recommend doing the long version once a month to start with for a few months before trying the shortened version. To do the shortened version you will need to have the resources for this exercise ready to use. I keep the resources in a small plastic box and find a fold-out gardening table which extends and is the best surface to use. I keep this folded up when not in use, and it take two minutes to unfold and extend ready to use. I wipe it clean afterwards and it doesn't matter if paint gets splattered on it.

The image I use for this exercise is the labyrinth or maze. The labyrinth is a symbol of the Quest in its many forms. The Quest is for what has been lost, one's own soul or essential Self. There is only one path which leads eventually to numerous experiences where one is forced to make constant choices. This endless confrontation with new experiences and choices constitute the labyrinth within which we must search for meaning and direction and ultimately find the Path of Liberation leads out of the labyrinthian life (from Finley Eversole, 'Art and Spiritual Transformation: The Seven Stages of Death and Rebirth', in A. Seyderhelm, *Coming to My Senses: Finding My Voice through Ovarian Cancer*, 2012).

The original inspiration for this painting practice came from Suzette Clough's Visual Medicine technique which she calls 'no brush painting' (Clough, 2012).

What you are going to do
Paint 20 small paintings over a 30-minute period.

What you will need

- 1 pack of Indian Khadi paper.
- 1 plastic container to use as a water bucket to wet your paper.
- Jam jars, each one filled with the primary colours mixed to a thickish pouring consistency.
- A single plastic sheet A3 size.
- A table mat to use as a paint mixing board.

This is an example of the type painting that is done during the Quest painting exercise.

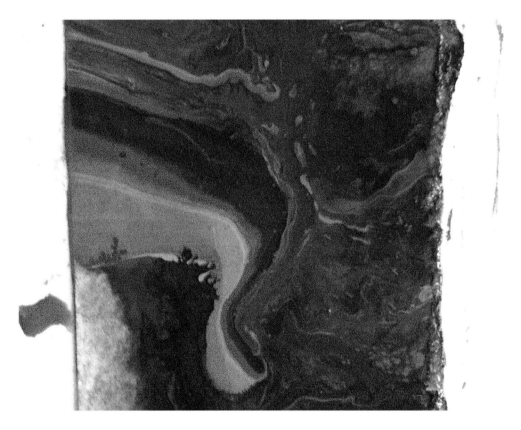

No brush painting method
Place the plastic sheet on the floor or table. Set your table mat on the floor or table, in front of you. Fill your water bucket with water. Place your Khadi papers (you should have 20 small pieces about A5 size) into the water. Shake and then uncap your jars of paint. Select three colours and pour a large blob of paint onto the table mat. Select a piece of wet paper and touch the edges of the paint with this. With your free hand pick up the table mat so that the paint moves onto the paper and just play with the movement of the paint. When you have enough paint on the paper, put the table mat down and spend time moving the paper around, watching the wet paint drizzle and dribble around the paper. Notice the shapes and feelings that are aroused in you while you are doing this. When you are happy with the painting, set

this down on the plastic sheet in front of you. Repeat this exercise until you have completed all 20 paintings.

I like to play music while completing this exercise as this can change your mental state so that you are more receptive to the colours and textures, feeling the paint on your hands, noticing how getting messy makes you feel! Some people love this and others don't. Just notice how you feel.

Take 15 minutes to write in your notebook what the experience felt like.

Things to pay attention to: patterns and themes which recur in the 20 paintings. Some people notice that once they have sat looking at the paintings and reflecting on their meaning, suddenly an idea of what they are about will come to them. This is important information to pay attention to, because it is coming from your higher self, what is sometimes called your spiritual self. This can give real significance to the whole Quest, and you may find that the meaning of the paintings stays with you for several days. I have had pupils feel quite transformed by doing this exercise. Old, stubborn patterns of thinking and behaviour can shift quickly while doing this exercise, so don't be surprised if you find yourself suddenly making connections. This is what we want! Write it all down in your notebook.

4. Whose story is this anyway?

Understanding how stories unlock mysteries of psychophysical suffering, and how to fix ineffective internalized stories.

Counter-transference is a therapeutic term used to describe a therapist's reaction to something a patient says … I think this actually happens all the time in schools, and if unchecked, it can leave teachers feeling like someone has just dumped a load of their backpack baggage onto them! This is certainly the feeling it generates in therapy, and when I teach this in social work and family support settings, everyone nods in recognition. I hear comments like 'I get fed up of hearing that story from X, it's nothing to do with me, why does he keep telling me, sounds like a stuck record.' If you have heard this kind of remark, it's good to pause and ask yourself why you are having such a strong reaction to hearing someone else's story. When you do this, you begin to understand more about the source of your reaction. For example, you might be triggered by hearing a story because it reminds you of a similar story which belongs to you or, someone close to you. Worst-case scenario is that sometimes if we seriously take on someone else's story it can make us ill, either physically or in a mental health way where we start to believe the narrative that actually belongs to someone else.

I have a simple exercise which I use at the start of my trainings which introduces the concept of transference without actually calling it that. Instead I call it, 'Whose story is this anyway?'

The reason I call it this is because it reminds me of the film *Whose Life Is It Anyway?* Ken Harrison (Richard Dreyfuss) is a well-known and respected sculptor, until a terrible car accident leaves him a paraplegic. His once positive outlook descends into depression as he comes to grips with the loss of his independence and his art. Even as he develops a relationship with Clare Scott (Christine Lahti), all he wants to do is end his life, but US law forbids assisted suicide. Dr Harrison (John Cassavetes) vows to keep Ken alive – while Ken's lawyer fights for his right to die.

The dominant narrative in the story is one which forbids Ken from asserting his right to die. Instead of accepting this, Ken fights for his own belief, which is to choose when he dies. In this regard, Ken takes back control of his life.

Sometimes other peoples' narratives impact us to the point where they can make us uncomfortable. When they do, we should ask if this is because we believe them or we don't.

What you are going to do

This is a therapeutic writing exercise.

You will need a selection of small objects, up to 20, which you are going to set out on a table in front of you. These objects can literally be anything. When I do this exercise I use the miniature objects that the children use in the sand tray but, it's unnecessary to go out and buy a whole load of these! In fact, it's more interesting in a way to use objects from your everyday life: stones, leaves and flowers from your garden, domestic objects from your home, just take a good look around and select the objects you like. I had one student who used a washing-up brush, and the story was so thoughtful, so allow yourself to be inspired when selecting the objects! This part of the exercise is a sort of fun part of the process itself, and interesting to reflect on afterwards in terms of the selection of objects. When you know you have time to do this exercise, allow time to collect your objects. For example, if you have a garden and want to use objects from it, allow time to take a walk through your garden and collect these. Be mindful while you are doing this, i.e. be present to the walk in your garden or, through your home, really take the time to look at each object, notice the colours and textures. All these objects will hold memories and stories for you which you will draw on in this exercise.

Once these are set up on the table, sit on a chair facing the objects, and spend a few moments looking at the objects. Choose one object from the table selection and hold this in your hands. Spend a few minutes looking at the object and notice how this makes you feel. Put the object on the floor and pick up your notebook.

Write the line 'Once upon a time, there was an object called X.' Give your object a name, and tell the object's story. Try not to edit yourself while writing, just write down whatever story comes to mind until you have completed one side of A4 paper. You must fill the page, so you don't need to set a timer for the writing part of the exercise because when you have written the whole page, you can stop.

Now, read the story out loud to yourself and really listen to the words you have used. Where does this resonate in your body? What feelings does this story arouse for you? Can you relate to this story, i.e. does it feel like yours or, is it one you have inherited from a loved one? We all internalize stories we have inherited from our parents and families and the skill here is knowing which ones are serving you and which ones aren't. When you have done this exercise a few times you will be amazed at how many of these internalized inherited stories you have all nicely packed away at the bottom of your backpack! Some of them maybe closer to the surface, as in the story is a common one you recognize because it's one that trips you up in relation to other people. Then, in your general conversations with colleagues, parents and children, you will become more attuned to the transference and counter-transference and find yourself silently saying to yourself: whose story is this anyway? And then smile.

5. Physical exercise

Yoga, dancing, Tai Chi, running, anything that gets your heart rate up and releases endorphins.

Final thoughts

I'm often asked about whether loss is different in different cultures. No. Loss is universal – heartbreak is heartbreak wherever and whoever you are. The human heart has no borders. Grief, however, is multicultural. For example, Eastern Orthodox Christians are expected to mourn their dead for up to 40 days after the funeral. Communities in many Islamic countries also practice a 40-day grieving period. In Judaism, the living sit shiva for a week to initially mourn their dead. Other days of remembrance are observed by some cultures. In Judaism, the anniversary of the death and the last day of the religious holiday Yom Kippur are reserved as days to remember loved ones. Whatever public face and ritual we have for coping with our loss and expressing our grief, heartbreak over losing someone we love hurts like hell because the dead aren't coming back to us, ever. And, however much we want to go back to our old home, school and friends, we can't because loss creates change and, learning to cope with that difference is what helps us to resolve the past and build our resilience.

I have treated children in my practice from different backgrounds, races, family dynamics and cultures and know *this* to be true: stories are the way in to a child's experience. They are door, mind and heart openers. And, once inside their own experience, children are able to run around, jump and play, fall down and get up again safely, viewing their heartbreak from both a safe and intimate distance. This 'exercise' gives them a pathway to make sense of their feelings. As adults it is easy to miss this awakening – after all, we have language and verbosity to express our feelings! The key here and, it's a vital one, is to recognize that the way we express our feelings and make sense of loss may be quite different from a child's way – our job, our one and only job, is to help children find that way, their own 'sense and sensibility', if you like.

A wise therapist and supervisor once said to me, after my Mum died and I had grieved my loss very hard: don't stay too long in your loss. At first I was upset by this remark because after all, nothing was ever going to be as devastating as losing my Mum. But she was right. Loss brings change, whether we like it or even want it, and nothing changes us like the death of a loved one. For children, making sense of the loss of a primary attachment figure can take years, decades even, and the hardest part is that there are no short-cuts to recovery and resilience. Whether we are all grown up or still in primary school, our best hope is that we can learn how to internalize the best of our departed and to take them with us, wherever we go.

My hope is that you will find some use for the stories in this book and discover your own way of sharing them with your children. Feel free to improvise while doing so – let the story take you to your own undiscovered places …

Final Thoughts

If you'd like to keep in touch and find out about events I'm hosting, readings and trainings, please check my website www.amandaseyderhelm.com and sign up for my quarterly newsletter. I'm on Twitter @TheKidDecoder and Facebook www.facebook.com/TheKidDecoder. I look forward to meeting you!

Amanda Seyderhelm
2020

Appendices

Appendix 1

The Red Flag list

Behaviour is a signal that something is either wrong or right. Behaviour is the child's way of waving a red flag in order to get your attention. These are the behaviours to be aware of in the classroom, because they may be indicating that the child is struggling with loss and change. Don't be too quick to raise the ADHD flag! I see this a lot in schools, and it's easy to conclude when the behaviour traits appear similar but, this does not mean the child has ADHD. First, check that the child has not experienced some type of loss or change.

Always focus on what is driving the behaviour rather than the behaviour itself, because that is where you start to build a connection with the child. This is why punishment/reward doesn't work. It may have the effect of stopping the behaviour but, it will not create meaningful nor lasting change for the child that has empathy and compassion at its heart.

- Deterioration in focus and concentration
- Being fidgety and unable to settle down to complete a task
- Jumping from one thing to another
- A sudden change in mood
- Angry outbursts
- Being unusually clingy
- Tiredness – yawning or falling asleep in class.

Appendix 2

The meaning of colours

White   – healing light, spiritual guidance, direction to the right path.
Red   – courage, energy, ability to take action, love, passion.
Yellow – power of the mind, mental creativity, confidence.
Orange – ability to change your luck and take control of your situation, energy.
Blue   – harmony, understanding, spiritual journey, loyalty, wisdom, protection.
Green   – balance, practical creativity, growth, health.
Brown   – defence, protection, counteraction, banishing evil.
Indigo – discovering past lives, sorting karmic problems, balancing karma, breaking repeating karmic patterns.
Purple – most powerful meditation colour, psychic and spiritual growth, healing, power, independence.

Appendix 3

Glossary

Acting out Exhibiting destructive behaviour that discharges the energy of your emotions, but results in negative consequences for yourself and others.

Adult Self The responsible part of yourself that governs your daily life.

Boundaries Personal boundaries are guidelines, rules or limits that people create to identify reasonable, safe and permissible ways for other people to behave towards them and how they will respond when someone passes those limits.

Centre of your being For most people this is the place in your body at the very bottom of your diaphragm. It is where your breath leads you when you inhale deeply.

Codependency An inability to fulfil your primary needs because your focus is always on meeting the needs of the person upon whom you are emotionally or financially dependent; ordinarily this is due to patterns of behaviour learned in childhood to ensure survival and that result in low self-esteem.

Developmental stages Predictable stages of emotional growth that occur in the natural progression from birth to adulthood. Each stage has specific tasks that need to be mastered if this progression is to occur successfully.

Guided imagery A structured imaginative fantasy whose purpose is to aid your internal exploration. You create images or scenes in your mind's eye and then relate to those images, directing them much as you would a play. Guided imagery does not always elicit visual responses; sometimes the scenes are evoked by recalling certain smells or tastes, or by hearing sounds of the scene being described.

Generalized grief Grief that extends beyond your personal experience; feeling the pain of others that is similar or the same as your own.

Higher power For some it is the image of a wise old being; for others is may be a sphere of light, a guardian angel or a spirit guide. For some it is experienced as part of the self; for others it will be something outside the self. The image may be based on religious beliefs, appearing in the form of Jesus, Buddha, Mohammed or a guru; others may experience it as an abstract symbol of a Higher Self such as a cross or a mandala, or the intuitive or spiritual part of self within you. Some may picture it as an aspect of nature, or a group to which one belongs.

Higher self The spiritual dimension of self.

Inherited grief Unresolved grief that is passed on from generation to generation until someone finally breaks the cycle and resolves the feelings of loss.

Inner child Small voices inside that carry childhood feelings.

Internal support group Supportive characters, real or imagined, that you bring into your guided imagery to support your exploration.

Journal A notebook that is used for personal reflections about your emotional and spiritual journey.

Mind's eye Your imagination; what you see in your head when you close your eyes and play imaginative scenes.

Processing Word used to describe the act of identifying, expressing and releasing feelings.

Protective light A healing light connected with your Higher Power that you call on imaginatively to aid your internal explorations; a metaphor for the healing power of the universal spirit.

Recovery The process of learning how to break addictive behaviour patterns and live with feelings non-addictively.

Ritual A ceremony performed for the purpose of celebrating the completion of a phase of your internal work or to provide a tangible way to release pain.

Self-esteem Describes your level of self-worth; how you feel about yourself. These feelings are based on how you were treated as a child. If you were treated with respect and you received love, you will have high self-esteem. If you were neglected, abused or abandoned you will have low self-esteem and not feel very worthy.

Support system Friends, family and others who believe in and encourage your personal growth.

Appendix 4

Exercise: Creative visualization: allow 20 minutes

This is a script which you can read out to the child.

Sit comfortably in a chair with your feet flat on the floor and your hands resting on your lap. Close your eyes. Relax your hands and feet and feel your body being held safely by the chair. Know that you are safe here in this space. Take a deep breath in through your nose and breathe out through your mouth. Repeat three times.

I want you to see before you a winding path in a forest. This forest is full of lush green trees and flowers. Now I want you to walk along your path until you come to an empty Well. This is your Worry Well into which you can throw all your worries. Pause a moment and write down your worries on a piece of paper. When you have finished writing down all your worries, screw up the piece of paper and throw them away into the Well. Watch them float down into the Well leaving you feeling lighter, and ready to move on. Now continue walking along your path. If you see any rocks or weeds in your path, stop and gently move them away. Send them your love before continuing on your path. Soon you will arrive at a small wooden door that is painted your favourite colour. Notice the welcome mat with your name on it as you gently push open the door. As you step through your door you enter into the most peaceful sanctuary you have ever seen. It is exactly the way you want it to be, and it is just for you. All the colours in your sanctuary are like precious stones. The sun is warm and glowing, and the ground is soft to walk on. The animals are playing happily together, and the birds are singing you a welcoming song. You feel safe and relaxed. Wander through your sanctuary and explore it … (Pause for a few minutes or for as long as your child's attention span holds) … Now, before you leave your sanctuary, I want you to thank your sanctuary for being there for you and for being exactly as you wanted it to be. Know that your sanctuary will always be there for you when you need it …

Count back slowly from 10 to 1, then tell the children to open their eyes and stretch their body.

Ask them to tell you about the experience. Listen for nuggets of information which tell you more about them.

Appendix 5

Assessment tool

I use Goodman's SDQ – Strengths and Difficulties Questionnaire for parental assessments.

These assessments are useful to complete with a child whom you are considering referring for specialist intervention like play therapy. They will also give you an insight into where the child's worries and anxieties are placed.

The Strengths and Difficulties Questionnaire (SDQ) – Rationale

Normally Play Therapy UK recommends the use of the Goodman's SDQ for measuring outcomes for the reasons described below.

In a child and adolescent mental health service it is important to accurately screen and measure children's emotional and behavioural problems. Traditionally many of the standardized self-report questionnaires developed to do this have been difficult to use in practice, as they have been long and have exclusively focused on problems and pathology, sometimes making them off-putting to parents, teachers and children to complete. This short note (based on Waldron, Sharry, Fitzpatrick, Behan and Carr, 2002), describes the shorter Strengths and Difficulties Questionnaire that measures prosocial as well as problematic behaviours and compares it to the traditional Child Behaviour Checklist (CBCL). A total of 65 parents (40 from a Dublin child mental health service and 25 from a Dublin school) completed both questionnaires. The results suggest moderate to high correlations between the measures on a range of subscales and support the claim that the shorter SDQ is a valid short measure for assessing and screening childhood behavioural and emotional problems.

The Strengths and Difficulties Questionnaire (SDQ, Goodman, 1997) is 'a brief behavioural screening questionnaire that provides balanced coverage of children and young people's behaviours, emotions and relationships'. 'The SDQ (informant version) asks about 25 attributes, 10 of which would generally be thought of as strengths, 14 of which would generally be thought of as difficulties, and one of which "gets on better with adults than other children" – is neutral' (Goodman, 1997a, p. 582). This neutral item is scored as a problem on the peer problem subscale. Items are scored on a 0 to 2 point scale reflecting parental attributions of Not True, Somewhat True and Certainly True respectively. Certain items on each subscale of the SDQ ask about behaviours or tendencies in a negative manner. Scores are reversed for these items.

Summing the 25 items of the scale generates scores for the 5 sub-scales.

> The scores for hyperactivity, emotional symptoms, conduct problems and peer problems can be summed to generate a total difficulties score ranging from 0 to 40; *the prosocial score is not incorporated in the reverse direction into the total difficulties score since the absence of prosocial behaviours is conceptually different from the presence of psychological difficulties* (Goodman, 1997a, p. 582).

Goodman and Scott (1999) wrote that the five items on the SDQ's inattention- hyperactivity scale

> were deliberately selected to tap inattention (2 items), hyperactivity (2 items) and impulsivity (1 item). These are the key symptom domains for a DSM-IV diagnosis of attention-deficit/ hyperactivity disorder (ADHD: American Psychiatric Association, 1994) or for an ICD-10 diagnosis of hyperkinesis (World Health Organisation, 1994). (Goodman and Scott, 1999, p. 17)

'The initial choice of items for the SDQ was guided by factor loadings and frequency distributions that had previously been obtained on an expanded Rutter parent questionnaire (Goodman, 1994): items were subsequently modified and amalgamated on the basis of a succession of informal trials as well as advice from colleagues' (Goodman, 1997a, p. 582). For example the expanded Rutter Questionnaire (Goodman, 1994) included ten prosocial items and three positive behaviour items. Following a factor analysis of these items and the original Rutter items a broadly positive/prosocial scale emerged. The seven items with the best loadings were amalgamated to become the subsequent five-item SDQ prosocial subscale.

The provisional banding for parent reported SDQ scores (Goodman, 1997b) *indicates that a cut-off score of 14 marks the lower boundary of the borderline range and a score of 17 is indicative of clinically significant abnormal difficulties.*

The SDQ has been reported to have high internal consistency (Goodman, Meltzer and Bailey, 1998; Smedje, Broman, Hetta, and von Knorring, 1999) and good test-retest reliability (Goodman and Scott, 1999). Similarly, a high discriminative validity in terms of high and low risk samples has been reported (Goodman and Scott, 1999). Factor analysis has supported the hypothesis that each of the five scales corresponds to a factor (Smedje et al., 1999). In addition, scores derived from the parent report version of the SDQ and Rutter parent questionnaire correlate highly with one another. The total score correlation was 0.88, the conduct problems correlation was 0.88. The emotional symptom correlation was 0.78 and the hyperactivity scale correlation was 0.82 (Goodman, 1997a).

References

This description is closely based on B. Waldron, J. Sharry, C. Fitzpatrick, J. Behan and A. Carr, 2002, 'Measuring children's emotional and behavioural problems: Comparing the Child Behaviour Checklist and the Strengths and Difficulties Questionnaire', *The Irish Journal of Psychology*, 23, 18–26.

Appendix 6

Template: Four-part pizza

As I advise throughout this book it's important to listen to the children and to understand the anxiety behind the behaviour, and to ask parents questions about the origin of this anxiety, because it's possible the children are being triggered at school by something which is rooted in their home life experience. This is a delicate tightrope for teachers to walk, but I believe that by asking a straightforward question, they may get more of the picture.

For example, are there any changes at home which might be causing the child anxiety? That may be enough for the parent to share what might be causing the child stress at home. However, very often, when I ask this question, I need to drill down and be specific, because the tendency is for teachers and parents to say no to this question, not out of defiance nor resistance, but because they may simply not know, and therefore need to ask their child.

Drilling down means asking two questions:

1. Has anyone close to your child died or moved away – in other words, has the child suffered any major loss? This will trigger them emotionally and potentially disrupt and deregulate them if that remains unacknowledged.
2. Do you fight in front of your children? How conflict is handled and resolved in a family usually holds the key to how secure a child feels. If they are witnessing their parents fight it is highly likely that they will also experience an emotional loss of security. Similarly, if conflict is treated with controlling behaviours such as threats, punishments, rewards, even silence, the child will get the message that having feelings is unsafe. This doesn't mean that the feelings will disappear, only that they will resurface somewhere else, usually at school, in inappropriate places, like the classroom, which then makes it the teacher's problem to resolve.

In my family play therapy practice I pay attention to how conflict is managed by spending time with the parents and helping them to understand how they are getting their needs met. The more we can get this dynamic dance to work the easier it will be for them to resolve conflict in ways that do not hurt the child's emotional health.

If the child is struggling to cope with feelings of loss and grief, they will also struggle to hold and contain themselves, as they react and respond emotionally from the right-side of their brain and this can result in the acting out behaviour. This may manifest at school as lashing out at other children and getting into fights and arguments, or being unable to accept boundaries or instructions in the classroom. If you find yourself describing a child as 'defiant', it is usually because somewhere they have an unmet emotional need which they are acting out through disobeying instructions – this is the child's way of bringing attention to their discomfort. This is the point at which you can take them aside and drill down until you get the Aha – the thing that is really upsetting them. At that point you can decide on the appropriate next steps. It may be enough for the child to have expressed his feelings to you directly and to have been heard. You will know this is the case if the child's behaviour improves. If it does not, that is the point at which to intervene again directly with the child by taking them aside and repeating the drill down process again. You may need to repeat this exercise several times until you have bottomed out the problem the child is struggling with. I find it helpful to use my backpack metaphor for this exercise.

When I train teachers, social workers and family support practitioners on how to use therapeutic play, one of the most popular concepts I teach is learning how to contain a child's difficult feelings. I start by asking them how they contain their own feelings. This is always an illuminating exercise for teachers, who usually realize that their personal containers are full to overflowing! It can be a painful yet useful realization, and we work then on creating strategies for them to deal with the full container, so they can decide what they want to keep and what they want to give back to someone else. For example, setting clearer boundaries, identifying 'whose need is this anyway', learning how to say no.

Template: Four-part pizza

Child: 4 part PIZZA

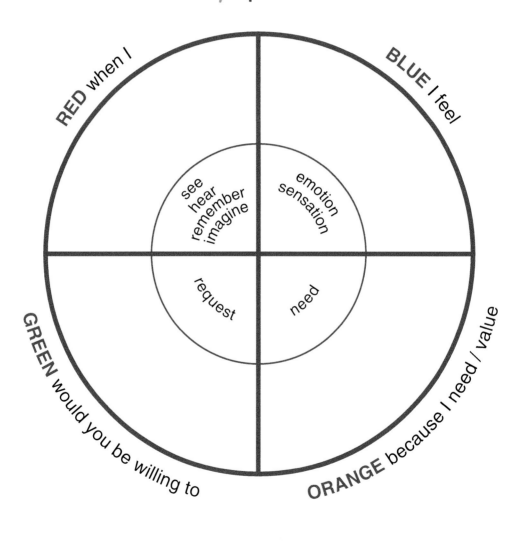

Appendix 7

Template: The frustration bubble

When children feel hurt as a result of experiencing a loss, what can happen is that they are dependent on the adults around them to help them to process that hurt. If the adults struggle themselves to do this, chances are that the children will also struggle. In this situation of struggle, the hurt may get covered up and the children will start to feel frustrated and irritable. They may experience tummy aches or headaches as their bodies struggle to express their feelings. This tension builds up until it gets expressed as anger. This is when it's a red flag for the teacher, who may see the children acting out angrily in the classroom. This is the moment to take the children out into a quiet space and use one of the Appetizer or Main Course exercises to bring their temperature down so that they can start to let go of their frustration and start to process the hurt that's actually driving the behaviour and is at the root cause.

The frustration bubble represents the way in which children can feel 'fit to burst' when their feelings are not being fully acknowledged nor expressed. Until then they might act out and have angry outbursts and melt downs. Once they are, the bubble reduces and an easier flow is created for the child.

You can use the template below with children and ask them to name the feelings they have in their tummy.

Appendix 8

Backpack stick figure template

Appendix 9

Unpacking the adult backpack exercise

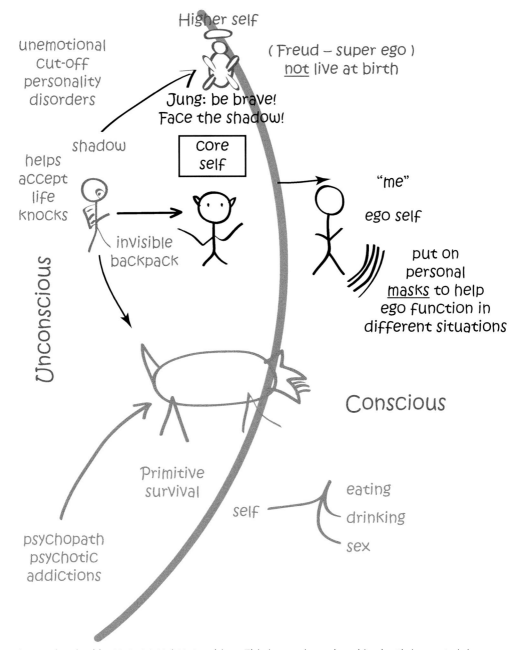

Image inspired by Kate McKairt's teaching. This image is explored in depth in my trainings.

This diagram presents how the conscious and unconscious self function to protect and obscure the core and higher self, our best self. It shows how the ego wears masks to help the ego function in different situations and how the Shadow self presents both an opportunity for growth or emotional cut off.

In my trainings, delegates are invited to use creative arts to explore questions relating to their identity and the different roles they play, to help them step away from their analytical brain and play, as the children do: they make masks and explore what it feels like to wear them and remove them. Doing this helps them to find the answers to these deep questions.

This type of work is deep and searching and consequently touches some rough and painful places. It is therefore best done in small facilitated therapeutic groups where delegates are properly supported and navigated through each step.

I have distilled these longer exercises into six steps which you can do either by yourself or, with a buddy. These steps could be completed during an afternoon.

Step 1: Make five masks using paper plates, and decorate these with crafts: the ego, primitive self, core self, shadow self and higher self. Wear these masks individually as you walk around a room, getting into the character of each mask. For example, when you are wearing your shadow mask, you might feel angry, irritable. Just notice how you feel.

Steps 2–6 are therapeutic writing exercises for you to complete in your notebook:

Step 2: What is the origin of this feeling/belief/fear, etc.?
Step 3: How is this mask serving me? What do I get out of holding it? What is the payoff?
Step 4: What am I willing to risk changing to feel differently?
Step 5: What does that change look and feel like?
Step 6: What type of support do I need to help me make this change.

In the classroom it is can be challenging to hold and contain an angry child who is disrupting the class. Sometimes a period of therapy is necessary to help the child if these angry outbursts become too disruptive. However, before referring the child onto a therapist use the exercises in this book to bring the emotional temperature down.

Appendix 10

How to set up the classroom Craft Station to enhance emotional literacy in coping with loss and change

The purpose of this is to create a dedicated station where children can have therapeutic 'time in'. Grief can sometimes cause sensory overload in children and make it difficult for them to focus and concentrate on their school work; they may distract other children as well. Instead of taking them out of the classroom to attend a separate intervention, the dedicated Craft Station gives them 'time in' to offload some of their difficult feelings. This means that the teacher can set their task, from a prescribed list of themes, and check in with them during her class. It's important to set a time limit around the 'time in', 15 minutes at most.

This is not a free-for-all in terms of allowing the children to do whatever they like at the Craft Station. To set this up, it's a good idea to explain the Craft Station to all the children which will bring a greater awareness and enhancement of their emotional vocabulary and literacy. It can also create a classroom culture of respect, trust and cooperation, when the children see how useful the Craft Station is.

It's a good idea to tell the children that the Craft Station is in use only at certain times of the day so that they recognize the boundary around it in terms of time and usage and don't try to use this anytime. Knowing this will also help them to hold and contain their worries that are making their backpack feel heavy.

Weekly themes

Each week you could set a craft theme. Some suggestions are:

- Dreamcatchers
- A Wishing Well Tree (this could either be an individual tree or, a class tree)
- Memory cards, in memory of a loved one
- Comfort creatures, animals and fish out of paper plates.

Developmentally appropriate activities

The most important aspect of this role is to work in a child-centred way, and to be open to working with the children in whatever way their capabilities allow. This might involve helping them to hold a pencil, showing them how to use the materials (younger children like using the dabbing paints), and letting them lead the craft creation as much as possible once you have set this up and explained what to do. I have found that most children like having some structure rather than a blank page which can seem daunting, so you can give them part of the craft to create while you work on the other part, and in this way you are working together while also encouraging them to put their own personality into the craft.

Freedom of choice fosters creativity

There is no right nor wrong in the craft creations. If once you have explained how to make the craft the child chooses to make it differently, gently follow them and be open to what they are creating. You may be surprised!

Encouragement not criticism

Children who are grieving may be in an emotionally heightened state, so it's important to always encourage them in what they are creating, and to congratulate them when they finish (or want to stop) making the craft. We want them to leave the Craft Station feeling positive about their experience, and as a relaxed as possible as they go back to their classroom activities.

Discussions and interactive conversations

Some children will talk about their loss, and it's important to listen attentively, and not bombard them with questions. Let them talk, as this is a chance for them to offload their worries and anxieties, and helps divert them from stress. Be compassionate at all times. If you are concerned about something a child has disclosed, tell the child's parent/caregiver immediately. If this is a safeguarding issue, follow the school's safeguarding policy.

Keeping the crafts

The children can show their completed craft work to peers, or they might like to take it home to show their family. Sometimes they may want to give this to their teacher or classroom assistant. Always invite the children to keep the crafts that they make. If children want you to keep the craft for them, explain that the craft will be left on the table for them to collect until the end of the day.

DON'TS

Give young children scissors! Always cut something for them, and then return the scissors to the trolley.

The Craft Station themes
Animals and butterflies

Skills: choosing colours, drawing, cutting out, sticking, pasting

Demonstrate how to draw figures, and the children can then draw their own; we cut them out of paper plates, and the children can decorate them and make collages and add their name to personalize their craft.

Dream catchers

Skills: drawing circles, cutting out and sticking, choosing different paper textures

This can be an individual or group activity. In a group the children will usually start to help each other, and become curious about what each one is making. Encourage the children to come up with solutions, and experiment with other ideas, to truly make the dreamcatchers their own.

The wishing tree

Skills: choosing colours, drawing, cutting out, sticking, writing

Draw the outline of a tree with bare branches and invite the children to add their wishes to the branches. This theme works particularly well with loss because it allows the children to directly express their wishes. Don't worry how magical some of these wishes are.

Underwater sea world

Skills: choosing paper texture, choosing colours, cutting out, sticking, pasting

Drawing sea creatures freehand and pasting them onto a piece of paper; drawing templates and cutting these out for children to colour in: dolphins, starfish, octopus, boats, mermaids.

Disney characters

Skills: colouring in, socialization, parental collaboration

Children elected to colour in Disney characters that were printed out as templates. Lots of group discussion about their favourite films and characters. Lots of energy and group social interaction with parents.

Visual storytelling asking six questions

Skills: imagination, drawing, writing, choosing colours

Introduce visual storytelling using six boxes on an A3 card and ask the six questions as they draw pictures in each box.

Superheroes

Skills: imagination, choosing colours, drawing, interacting

Hulk, Superman, Supergirl and Captain America.

Blossoming

Skills: choosing paper textures, choosing colours, cutting out, sticking, pasting

Flowers, gardens and garlands.

Changing seasons and trees

Skills: hand/eye coordination, drawing, colouring, cutting, pasting

Make trees out of brown paper bags, and cut out glitter petals which the children can use to decorate their trees in different colours.

Hand prints

Skills: colour selection, drawing, parental collaboration, socialization

Use the autumn season of falling leaves, and invite the children to draw their own hand print, and decorate these. A simple craft which each child can personalize. Very popular with all age groups.

Resources

Adoption

Good, common-sense resources are available to parents. Lois Melina's *Making Sense of Adoption: A Parent's Guide* is an excellent, practical source of adoption information for parents. Joyce Maguire Pavao's *The Family of Adoption* looks at the entire family's adoption experience throughout the family life cycle. Lois Melina's 'Talking to children about their adoption: When to start, what to say, what to expect', is a brief, yet informative, article for parents that was published in the *Adopted Child* newsletter.

Divorce

Action for Children
Support families through divorce, bereavement and children's behavioural problems.

Citizens Advice Bureau
Your local branch is listed in the telephone directory.

Divorce Aid
Run by an independent group of professionals, it provides advice, support and information on all aspects of divorce. It has specialized sections for both young children and teenagers, enabling them to recognize and deal with emotions that arise from separation and divorce.

Family Lives
Parentline offers help and advice to parents on bringing up children and teenagers: tel. 0808 800 2222.

National Family Mediation
An organization specifically set up to help families who are separating. It has a useful booklist, which includes books for children of different ages.

Relate
Offers a range of services to help families and couples going through separation and divorce.

The Children's Society
Produces a series of leaflets for children and parents.

The Money Advice Service
Information and advice on the financial aspects of divorce, separation or civil partnership dissolution, including an interactive calculator to help manage finances, work put what you have and owe, and consider how you might split what you have.

Bereavement

CRUSE: https://www.cruse.org.uk/
The Laura Centre: www.thelauracentre.org.uk
Childhood Bereavement UK: https://www.childbereavementuk.org/
Winstons Wish: https://www.winstonswish.org/
Amanda Seyderhelm: http://www.amandaseyderhelm.com

Bibliography

Print sources

Abrams, J. (1990). *Reclaiming the Inner Child*. Los Angeles: Jeremy P. Tarcher.

Achenbach, T. (1991). *Integrative Guide for the 1991 CBCL 4–18, YSR, and TRF profiles*. Burlington, VT: University of Vermont.

Achenbach, T.M. and Edelbrook, C.S. (1983). *Manual for the Child Behaviour Checklist and Revised Child Behaviour Profile*. Burlington, VT: University Associates in Psychiatry.

American Psychiatric Association. (1994). *Diagnostic and Statistical Manual of Mental Disorders* (4th edn). Washington, DC: APA.

Axline, V. (1969). *Play Therapy*. New York: Ballantine.

Bacon, R.L. (1988). *Hemi and the Whale*. Auckland: Waiatarua Publishing.

Barnsley (1997). *Dancing on the Grave: Encounters with Death*. London: Abacus.

Berg, I., Lucas, C. and McGuire, R. (1992). 'Measurement of behaviour difficulties in children using standard scales administered to mothers by computer: Reliability and validity'. *European Child and Adolescent Psychiatry*, 1, 14–23.

Bettelheim, B. (1991). *The Uses of Enchantment: The Meaning and Importance of Fairy Tales*. London: Penguin.

Boffey, D. (2014). 'Children's hyperactivity "is not a real disease"', *The Guardian*, 30 March.

Boss, P. (2006). *Loss, Trauma and Resilience: Therapeutic Work with Ambiguous Loss*. New York: W. W. Norton.

Bowlby, J. (1998). *Attachment and Loss*, Vol. 3: *Loss: Sadness and Depression*. London: Pimlico.

Brodzinsky, D. (ed). (1990). *The Psychology of Adoption*. Oxford: Oxford University Press.

Brodzinsky, D.M., Schechter, M.D. and Marantz Hening, R. (1992). *Being Adopted: The Lifelong Search for Self*. New York: Doubleday.

Cacciatore, J. (2017). *Bearing the Unbearable: Love, Loss and the Heartbreaking Path of Grief*. Somerville, MA: Wisdom Publications.

Cantor, M.D. (2007). *The Use of Storytelling in Therapy with Children*. Northampton, MA: Smith College School for Social Work.

Christ, G.H. (2000). *Healing Children's Grief: Surviving a Parent's Death from Cancer* (New edn). New York: Oxford University Press.

Clough, S. (2012). *Visual Art: The Art of the Unknown*. Visual Medicine Publications.

Combs, G. and Freedman, J. (1990). *Symbol, Story and Ceremony: Using Metaphor in Individual and Family Therapy*. New York: W. W. Norton & Company, Inc.

Crenshaw, D.A. (1999). *Bereavement: Counselling the Grieving throughout the Life Cycle.* Eugene.

Derdeyn, A. and Graves, C.L. (1998.) 'Clinical vicissitudes of adoption'. *Child Adolesc Psychiatry North Am.*, 7, 373–388.

Elander, J. and Rutter, M. (1996). 'Use and development of the Rutter parents' and teachers' scales'. *International Journal of Methods in Psychiatric Research*, 6, 63–78.

Figley, C.R. (1995). 'Compassion Fatigue: Toward a New Understanding of the Costs of Caring'. In B.H. Stamm (ed.), *Secondary Traumatic Stress: Self-care Issues for Clinicians, Researchers, and Educators* (pp. 3–28). Baltimore, MD: The Sidran Press.

Fombonne, E. (1989). 'The Child Behaviour Checklist and the Rutter Parental Questionnaire: A comparison between two screening instruments'. *Psychological Medicine*, 19, 777–785.

Fox, S. (1985). 'Psychological Tasks of Grief'. In S. Fox, *Good Grief: Helping Groups of Children when a Friend Dies.* Boston, MA: The New England Association for the Education of Young Children.

Fraga, J. (2017). 'When a pet dies: Helping children through the worst day of their lives', *New York Times*, 8 June.

Freud, S. (1917/2005*). On Murder, Mourning and Melancholia.* London: Penguin.

Furman, E. (1981). *A Child's Parent Dies: Studies in Childhood Bereavement.* New Haven, CT: Yale University Press.

Gersie, A. (1992). *Storymaking in Bereavement: Dragons Fight in the Meadow.* London: Jessica Kingsley Publishers.

Gersie, A. (1997). *Reflections on Therapeutic Storymaking: The Use of Stories in Groups.* London: Jessica Kingsley Publishers.

Goodman, R. (1994). 'A modified version of the Rutter Parental Questionnaire including items on children's strengths: A research note'. *Journal of Child Psychology and Psychiatry*, 35, 1483–1494.

Goodman, R. (1997a). 'The Strengths and Difficulties Questionnaire: A research note'. *Journal of Child Psychology and Psychiatry*, 38, 581–586.

Goodman, R. (1997b). The Strengths and Difficulties Questionnaire information sheet. London: Goodman.

Goodman, R. and Scott, S. (1999). 'Comparing the Strengths and Difficulties Questionnaire and the Child Behaviour Checklist: Is small beautiful?' *Journal of Abnormal Child Psychology*, 27, 17–24.

Goodman, R., Meltzer, H. and Bailey, V. (1998). 'The Strengths and Difficulties Questionnaire: A pilot study of the validity of the self-report version'. *European Child and Adolescent Psychiatry*, 7, 125–130.

Halprin, D. (2003). *The Expressive Body in Life, Art and Therapy: Working with Movement, Metaphor and Meaning.* London: Jessica Kingsley Publishers.

Heegard, M. (1991). *When Someone Very Special Dies.* Minneapolis, MN: Woodland Press.

Hillman, J. (1997). *Suicide and the Soul.* Woodstock, CT: Spring Publications.

Hillman, J. and Pozzo, L. (1983). *Inter Views: Conversations with Laura Pozzo on Psychotherapy, Biography, Love, Soul, Dreams, Work, Imagination, and the State of the Culture.* New York: Harper & Row.

Hinkle, D.E., Wiersma, W. and Jurs, S.G. (1994). *Applied Statistics for the Behavioural Sciences.* Boston: Houghton Mifflin Company.

Holland, J. (2001). *Understanding Children's Experiences of Parental Bereavement.* London: Jessica Kingsley.

Jennings, S. (1999). *Introduction to Developmental Playtherapy, Playing and Health*. London: Jessica Kingsley Publishers.

Jewett Jaratt, C. (1994). *Helping Children Cope with Separation and Loss*. Boston: The Harvard Common Press.

Jung, C.J. (1958). *Psyche and Symbol*. New York: Doubleday.

Jung, C.J., von Franz, M.-L., Henderson, Joseph L., Jaffé, A. and Jacobi, J. (1964). *Man and his Symbols*. New York: Doubleday.

Kasius, M., Ferdinand, R., van den Berg, H. and Verhulst, F. (1997). 'Associations between different diagnostic approaches for child and adolescent psychopathology'. *Journal of Child Psychology and Psychiatry*, 38, 625–632.

Klass, D. (2001). 'The Inner Representations of the Dead Child in the Psychic and Social Narratives of Bereaved Parents'. In R.A. Neimeyer (ed.), *Meaning Reconstruction and the Experience of Loss* (pp. 77–94). Washington, DC: American Psychological Association.

Kubler-Ross, E. (1982). *On Death & Dying: What the Dying Have to Teach Doctors, Nurses, Clergy & Their Own Families*. New York: Scribners.

Landreth, G. (2002). *Play Therapy: The Art of the Relationship*. New York: Brunner-Routledge.

Maguire Pavao, J. (1998). *The Family of Adoption*. Boston: Beacon Press.

Malchiodi, C.A. (2007). *The Art Therapy Sourcebook*. New York: McGraw-Hill.

Melina, L. (1989). *Making Sense of Adoption: A Parent's Guide*. New York: Harper Collins.

Melina, L. (1998). *Raising Adopted Children: Practical Reassuring Advice for Every Adoptive Parent*. New York: HarperCollins Publishers Inc.

Melina, L. (2000). 'Talking to children about their adoption: When to start, what to say, what to expect'. *Adopted Child*, 19, 1–4.

Mellon, N. (2000). *Storytelling with Children*. Stroud: Hawthorn Press.

Mills, J.C. and Crowley, R. (1986). *Therapeutic Metaphors for Children and the Child Within*. London: Brunner-Routledge.

Mills, J.C. and Crowley, R.J. in collaboration with Ryan, M.O. (2001). *Therapeutic Metaphors for Children and the Child Within*. New York: Brunner-Routledge.

Neimeyer, R.A. (2000). 'Searching for the meaning of meaning: Grief therapy and the process of reconstruction'. *Death Studies*, 24(6), 541–558.

Oishi, S. and Schimmack, U. (2010). 'Residential mobility, well-being, and mortality'. *Journal of Personality and Social Psychology*, 98(6), 980–994.

Okun, B.F. and Anderson, C.M. (1996). *Understanding Diverse Families: What Practitioners Need to Know*. New York: Guilford Press.

Parkes, C.M. (2010). *Studies of Grief in Adult Life*. London: Penguin.

Pfifferling, J. and Gilley, K. (2000). 'Overcoming compassion fatigue'. *Family Practice Management*, 7(4), 39–44.

Rutter, M. (1996). 'Stress Research: Accomplishments and Tasks Ahead'. In R.J. Haggerty, L.R. Sherrod, N. Garmezy and M. Rutter (eds), *Stress, Risk, and Resilience in Children and Adolescents: Processes, Mechanisms, and Interventions* (pp. 354–385). New York: Cambridge University Press.

Rutter, M. (1967). 'A children's behaviour questionnaire for completion by teachers: Preliminary findings'. *Journal of Child Psychology and Psychiatry*, 8, 1–11.

Sandler, I.N. et al. (2010). 'Long-term effects of the family bereavement program on multiple indicators of grief in parentally bereaved children and adolescents'. *Journal of Consulting and Clinical Psychology*, 78(2), 131–143.

Sandler, I.N. et al. (2013). 'Family bereavement program (FBP) approach to promoting resilience following the death of a parent'. *Family Science*, 4(1), 87–94.

Shacham, M. and Lahad, O.A.M. (2012). *The "BASIC Ph" Model of Coping and Resiliency: Theory, Research and Cross-Cultural Application*. London: Jessica Kinglsey.

Sharry, J. and Fitzpatrick, C. (1997). *Parents Plus Programme: A Practical and Positive Video-based Course for Managing and Solving Discipline Problems in children*. Manual and videos. Dublin: Department of Child and Family Psychiatry, Mater Misericordiae Hospital.

Silverman, P.R. and Kelly, M. (2009). *A Parent's Guide to Raising Grieving Children: Rebuilding Your Family after the Death of a Loved One* (1st edn). Oxford and New York: Oxford University Press.

Silverman, P.R. and Klass, D. (1996). *Continuing Bonds: New Understandings of Grief*. Philadelphia, PA: Taylor & Francis.

Smedje, H., Broman, J.E., Hetta, J. and von Knorring, A.L. (1999). 'Psychometric properties of a Swedish version of the Strengths and Difficulties Questionnaire'. *European Journal of Child and Adolescent Psychiatry*, 8, 63–70.

Stroebe, M. and Schut, H. (1999). 'The dual process model of coping with bereavement: Rationale and description'. *Death Studies*, 23(3), 197–224.

Stroebe, W. and Stroebe, M. (1987.) *The Psychological and Physical Consequences of Partner Loss*. Cambridge: Cambridge University Press.

Sunderland, M. (2001). *A Pea Called Mildred: A Story to Help Children Pursue Their Hopes and Dreams* (Helping Children with Feelings Series). Oxford: Speechmark Publishing.

Sunderland, M. (2003). *Using Story Telling as a Therapeutic Tool with Children*. Oxford: Speechmark Publishing.

Sveen, J., Eilegård, A., Steineck, G. and Kreicbergs, U. 2014, 'They still grieve—a nationwide follow-up of young adults 2–9 years after losing a sibling to cancer'. *Psychooncology*, 23(6), 658–664.

Walter, T. (1996). 'A new model of grief: Bereavement and biography'. *Mortality*, 1(1), 7–25.

Ward, B. (1993). *Healing Grief: A Guide to Loss and Recovery*. London: Vermilion.

Waters, T. (2004). *Therapeutic Storywriting: A Practical Guide to Developing Emotional Literacy in Primary Schools*. Abingdon: Routledge.

Webb, R.T., Pedersen, C.B. and Mok, P.L.H. (2016). 'Adverse outcomes to early middle age linked with childhood residential mobility'. *American Journal of Preventive Medicine*, 51(3), 291–300.

Whitfield, C.L. (1983). *Boundaries and Relationships: Knowing, Protecting, and Enjoying the Self*. Deerfield Beach, FL: Health Communications Inc.

Wilkinson, M. (2006). *Coming into Mind: The Mind-Brain Relationship, a Jungian Perspective*. New York: Routledge.

Worden, W. (1991). *Grief Counselling and Grief Therapy*. New Haven, CT: Yale University Press.

Websites

Ages & Stages: Understanding Children's Anger. (no date). Available at: https://www.scholastic.com/teachers/articles/teaching-content/ages-stages-understanding-childrens-anger/ (Accessed: 4 July 2018).

ASU Professor's Bereavement Program to Roll out Nationwide. (2017). ASU Now: Access, Excellence, Impact. Available at: https://asunow.asu.edu/20171010-solutions-asu-profes sors-bereavement-program-roll-out-nationwide (Accessed: 7 July 2018).

Ayers, T.S. et al. (2013). 'The family bereavement program: Description of a theory-based prevention program for parentally-bereaved children and adolescents'. *Omega*, 68(4), 293–314. Available at: https://www.ncbi.nlm.nih.gov/pmc/articles/PMC4581530/ (Accessed: 7 July 2018).

Bunce, M. and Rickards, A. (2004). *Working with Bereaved Children: A Guide.* The Children's Legal Centre. Available at: https://www1.essex.ac.uk/armedcon/unit/projects/ wwbc_guide/index.html

Child Bereavement UK. (no date). Available at: www.elephantsteaparty.co.uk (Accessed: 30 August 2015).

Children and Young People's Emotional Responses. (2016). Cruse Bereavement Care. Available at: https://www.cruse.org.uk/Children/emotional-response#Anger (Accessed: 4 July 2018).

Davis, C. et al. (2000). *Searching for Meaning in Loss: Are Clinical Assumptions Correct?* Tavistock and Portman Library's collections. Available at: http://web.a.ebscohost.com/pfi/ detail/detail?vid=5&sid=43d52563-77af-4388-aef0-9ae48812c99f%40sessionmgr4006 &bdata=JmF1dGh0eXBlPXNoaWImc2l0ZT1wZmktbGl2ZQ%3d%3d#AN=353961& db=eoah (Accessed: 31 May 2018).

Ellin, A. (2018). 'When a sibling dies, or has a serious illness', *The New York Times*, 12 February. Available at: https://www.nytimes.com/2017/12/12/well/family/siblings-death-brother-sister-fatal-illness-disease.html (Accessed: 10 July 2018).

Fisher, J. (2011). *Psychoeducational Aids for Working with Psychological Trauma:* Harvard, Janina Fisher, Ph.D. Available at: https://janinafisher.com/flip-chart.html

Gardner, R. (1968). 'The mutual storytelling technique: Use in alleviating childhood Oedipal stories'. *Contemporary Psychoanalysis*, 4(2). Available at: www.tandfonline.com/doi/abs /10.1080/00107530.1968.10745136? journalCode=uucp20#.VeGcMnhsxIA (Accessed: 29 August 2015).

Guillaume, P. (1995). *Myth, Metaphor and Magic.* Available at: http://cat4chat.narod.ru

Helping Children Cope when a Caregiver Leaves. (no date). Available at: www. brighthorizons.com/family-resources/e-family-news/2003-when-caregivers-leave (Accessed: 9 July 2018).

Helping Children Say Goodbye to Teachers and Friends. (no date). Available at: www. brighthorizons.com/family-resources/e-family-news/2010-a-time-for-goodbyes/ (Accessed: 9 July 2018).

Hospice Education Institute. (no date). *Family Therapy.* Available at: https://www.hospiceuk. org/what-we-offer/publications (Accessed: 26 August 2015).

How Grief May Affect Children. (no date). Marie Curie. Available at: https://www.marie curie.org.uk/help/support/bereaved-family-friends/supporting-grieving-child/grief-affect-child (Accessed: 4 July 2018).

Klimek, C. (2015). *Grief, Loss and Bereavement.* Good Therapy. Available at: www. goodtherapy.org/therapy-for-grief.html#Models%20of%20Grief:%20Kubler-Ross,%20 Stroebe%20&%20Schut,%20and%20Worden (Accessed: 30 August 2015).

Moving is Tough for Kids. (no date). *Psychology Today.* Available at: www.psychologytoday. com/blog/thinking-about-kids/201007/moving-is-tough-kids (Accessed: 6 July 2018).

Murrell, A.A.J. (2016). *Is Moving Psychologically Dangerous for Children?* Safer America. Available at: http://safer-america.com/moving-psychologically-dangerous-children/ (Accessed: 6 July 2018).

Negash, S., and Sahin, S. (2011). 'Compassion fatigue in marriage and family therapy: Implications for therapists and clients'. *Journal of Marital and Family Therapy*, 37(1), 1–13. Retrieved from http://search.proquest.com/docview/846784972?accountid= 1229.

Paul, P. (2010) 'Moving house, marring young lives?', *The New York Times*, 9 July. Available at: https://www.nytimes.com/2010/07/11/fashion/11StudiedMoving.html (Accessed: 6 July 2018).

Sandberg, S. (2017). 'Opinion. Sheryl Sandberg: How to build resilient kids, even after a loss', *The New York Times*, 22 December. Available at: https://www.nytimes.com/2017/04/24/ opinion/sheryl-sandberg-how-to-build-resilient-kids-even-after-a-loss.html (Accessed: 7 July 2018).

Saying Goodbye to Preschool. (2012). Bright Horizons Parenting Blog. The Family Room. Available at: https://blogs.brighthorizons.com/familyroom/saying-goodbye-to-preschool/ (Accessed: 9 July 2018).

Schlossberg.pdf. (no date). Available at: www.unthsc.edu/students/wp-content/uploads/ sites/26/Schlossberg.pdf (Accessed: 9 July 2018).

Schwartz, A. (2016). *Grief, Grit, and Grace.* Dr. Arielle Schwartz. Available at: https://drari elleschwartz.com/grief-grit-and-grace-dr-arielle-schwartz/ (Accessed: 4 July 2018).

Seyderhelm, A. (2014). *Therapeutic Storytelling in Early Years Bereavement.* Available at: www.sueryder.org/Media-centre/Blog/2014/September/Early%20years%20loss%20 and%20bereavement (Accessed: 30 August 2015).

Simms, L. (2015). *A Harvest of Sorrow: All Things Healing.* Available at: www.allthingsheal ing.com/Storytelling/A-Harvest-of-Sorrow/16696#.VeBWi3hsxIA (Accessed: 28 August 2015).

Sims, D. (no date). *Anger and Grief in Children.* Available at: http://www.touchstonesongrief. com/touchstones/articles/Anger%20and%20Grief%20in%20Children.pdf

Smail, M. (2011). *Tribute to James Hillman. Sesame Institute Drama and Movement Therapy.* Available at: www.sesame-institute.org/psyche-hillman (Accessed: 29 August 2015).

Teachers Hating to Say Goodbye. (no date). *Psychology Today.* Available at: https://www. psychologytoday.com/blog/young-people-close/201603/teachers-hating-say-goodbye (Accessed: 9 July 2018).

The Impact of Divorce on Young Children and Adolescents. (no date). *Psychology Today.* Available at: www.psychologytoday.com/blog/surviving-your-childs-adolescence/201112/ the-impact-divorce-young-children-and-adolescents (Accessed: 23 June 2018).

The Transition from Pre-school to Primary School. (no date). Available at: https://thecren. com/index.php/blog/13-education/85-the-transition-from-preschool-to-primary-school-by-deborah-khan (Accessed: 9 July 2018).

Tyrell, M. (2013). *How to Create Stories for Therapy.* Available at: www.uncommon-know ledge.co.uk

UNICEF. (no date). *Goal: Reduce Child Mortality* Available at: https://www.unicef.org/mdg/ childmortality.html (Accessed: 4 July 2018).

Vogler, C. (1985). *A Practical Guide to Joseph Campbell's The Hero with a Thousand Faces.* The Writer's Journey. Available at: https://docs.google.com/document/d/1__UPZhimttsba_ 7kp30GnJN3rGFW0FSrWc0t4KO3cUI/edit (Accessed 26 July 2019).

What is Lost when a Parent Dies. (no date). *Psychology Today.* Available at: www.psycho logytoday.com/blog/raising-grieving-children/201008/what-is-lost-when-parent-dies (Accessed: 7 July 2018).

Whole_school_approach_to_lossandbereavement.pdf. (no date). Available at: https://www.seemescotland.org/media/8151/whole_school_approach_to_lossandbereavement.pdf (Accessed: 23 August 2018).

Wikipedia. (2015). *Archetypal Psychology*. Available at: https://en.wikipedia.org/wiki/Archetypal_psychology (Accessed: 29 August 2015).